Oleg Pomoshnikov

The MAS-15

Italian Navy Torpedo-armed Motorboat

KAGERO

Port side view of MAS-15. Mast stowed. Before the battle, the mast was retracted to the left side of the superstructure.

The limited basin of the Adriatic Sea favoured the operation of the light ships and various types of "microorganisms". The Italian naval command at the end of 1914 already drew attention to the combat capabilities of motor torpedo boats. The design of such a unit was presented in November, 1914, by the Italian company Maccia Marchini. The cutter had a displacement of 7–8 tons, a length of 15 meters and was propelled by two engines, 200 HP each. It was supposed to reach a speed of 30 knots. The armament was two torpedoes dropped from both sides. However, the Italian Navy decided not to work with a small and not very well-known company.

The fate of the project proposed in February, 1915, by the Venetian company SVAN (Società Veneziana Automobili Nautiche – Venetian Society of Self-Propelled Sea Boats) was different. Torpedo boat designed by engineer Atillia Bisio was somewhat reminiscent of the design of the Maccia Marchini company. It had a similar displacement (7.8 tons) and a length of 15 meters. The drive consisted of four engines with a power of 100 HP each, working on two propeller shafts. The armament was limited to two 450 mm torpedoes and one 37 mm gun.

After making corrections to the design, the fleet ordered two torpedo boats on 5th of March, 1915. They received the designation MAS (Motobarca Armata SVAN – SVAN armed motor boat). The boats were to be ready the same year. To meet the requirements of the fleet, the dimensions and displacement were enlarged, also engine power was increased to 220 HP. These were 6-cylinder Isotta-Fraschini L-56 petrol engines. Torpedoes were fired from the stern's channel launchers.

Two experimental boats: MAS-1 and MAS-2 had better seaworthiness and a longer range of operation. However, the test results of these units did not satisfy the Italian naval command. As a result, it gave up the idea of building torpedo boats, and the two above-mentioned units were converted into miners with four mines, a 47 mm gun and two machine guns.

Without waiting for the completion of the tests of the first two MAS-1 and MAS-2 torpedo boats, the Italian fleet command entrusted SVAN with the design and construction of an anti-submarine motor boat. The requirements were as follows: speed of not less than 25 knots and armament consisting of a 57 mm caliber cannon and depth charg-

12-ton SVAN cutters [public domain]

Battleship "Szent István" at the Pola base, followed by "Viribus Unitis" and "Tegetthof", 1916 [WLB Stuttgart]

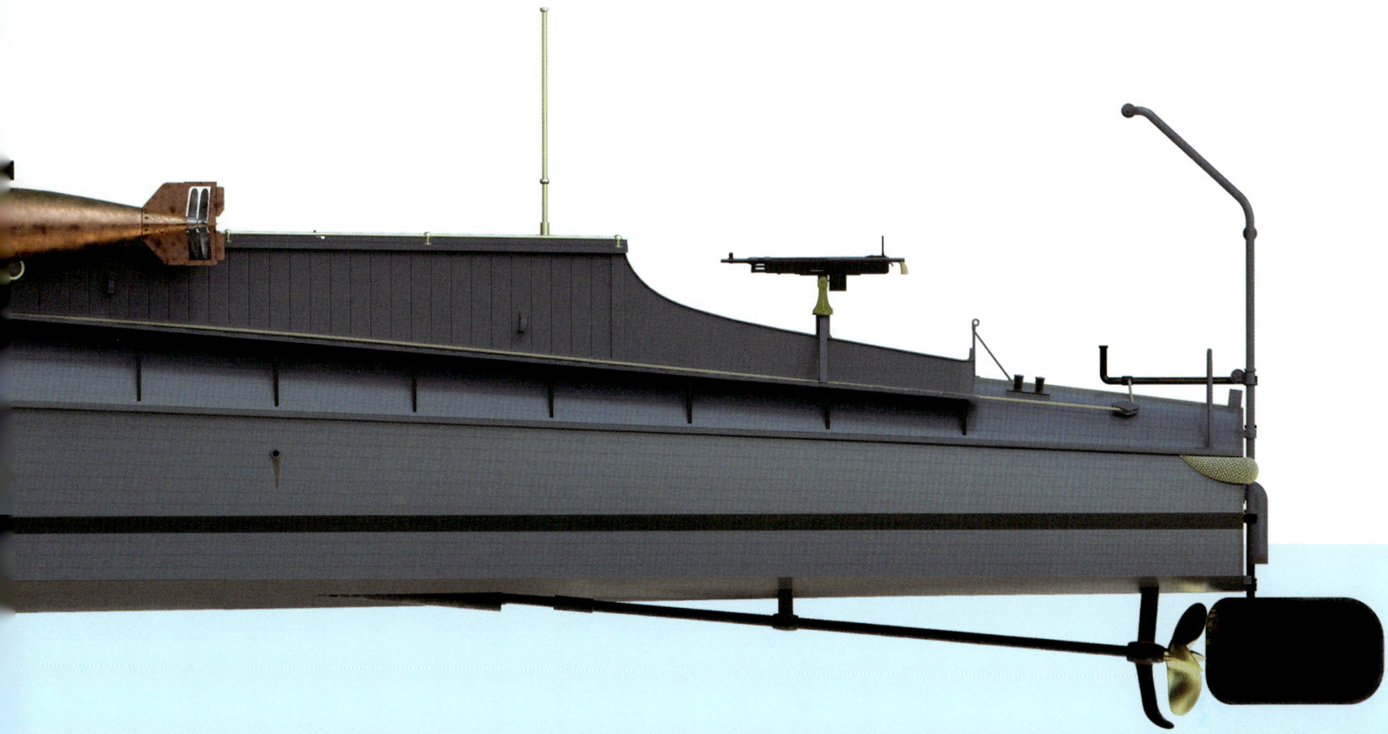

es. The SVAN company quickly developed a project of a cutter with a displacement of 4.8 tons and an engine power of 150 HP. This design was rejected due to its low seaworthiness and small size hampering the effective use of the weapon. At the same time, the fleet gave the constructors specific requirements: a strong 15-meter hull (similar to the flat-bottomed hull of the MAS 1 and MAS-2), good seaworthiness, a strong and reliable engine ensuring a speed of not less than 25 knots, fuel supply ensuring a 200-mile range cruising at maximum speed. The armament consisted of one 57 mm cannon with a 360° firing sector, two 6.5 mm machine guns and 6 depth charges. The project was approved by the fleet command and on 16th of July, 1915, SVAN received an order to build 20 cutters. The displacement of these wooden hulls units was 9.25 tons, and the propulsion was provided by airline gasoline L-56 engines from the already known company Isotta – Fraschini. Despite the approval, the design was subject to constant changes, which led to an increase in the displacement to 11.4 tons. This in turn resulted in a reduction of the maximum speed to 21–22 knots. In order to meet the timely delivery of the boats, several other Venetian shipyards had to be involved in their construction. Nevertheless, the entire series of 20 units (MAS-3–MAS-22) was not completed until the end of 1916. The first five cutters (MAS-3–MAS-7) were completed in anti-submarine version (Motobarca anti-sommergibili – anti-submarine motorboat).

In the spring of 1916, after the completion of the MAS-3 marching tests, the attitude of the Italian command changed and the idea of a torpedo boat was abandoned. It was decided to use some of the boats of this series as a torpedo units. The proximity of the main bases of the Austro-Hungarian fleet (Pula, Trieste and Cattaro) to the Italian military ports encouraged attempts to attack the enemy ships stationed there. The next boats of this series: MAS-8–MAS-22 have already been completed in the torpedo version (Motobarca Armata Silurante – motorized armoured torpedo boat). It coincided with the study by engineer Bisio of a new method of side-dropping the torpedoes (called ring). With this method, the torpedoes were held by gripper holders located on both sides. In the marching position, the torpedoes were lying on the cutter's deck, along the sides. When the

Luigi Rizzo – Italian national hero [public domain]

MAS-15 in march with two torpedoes on board [WLB Stuttgart]

Starboard view.

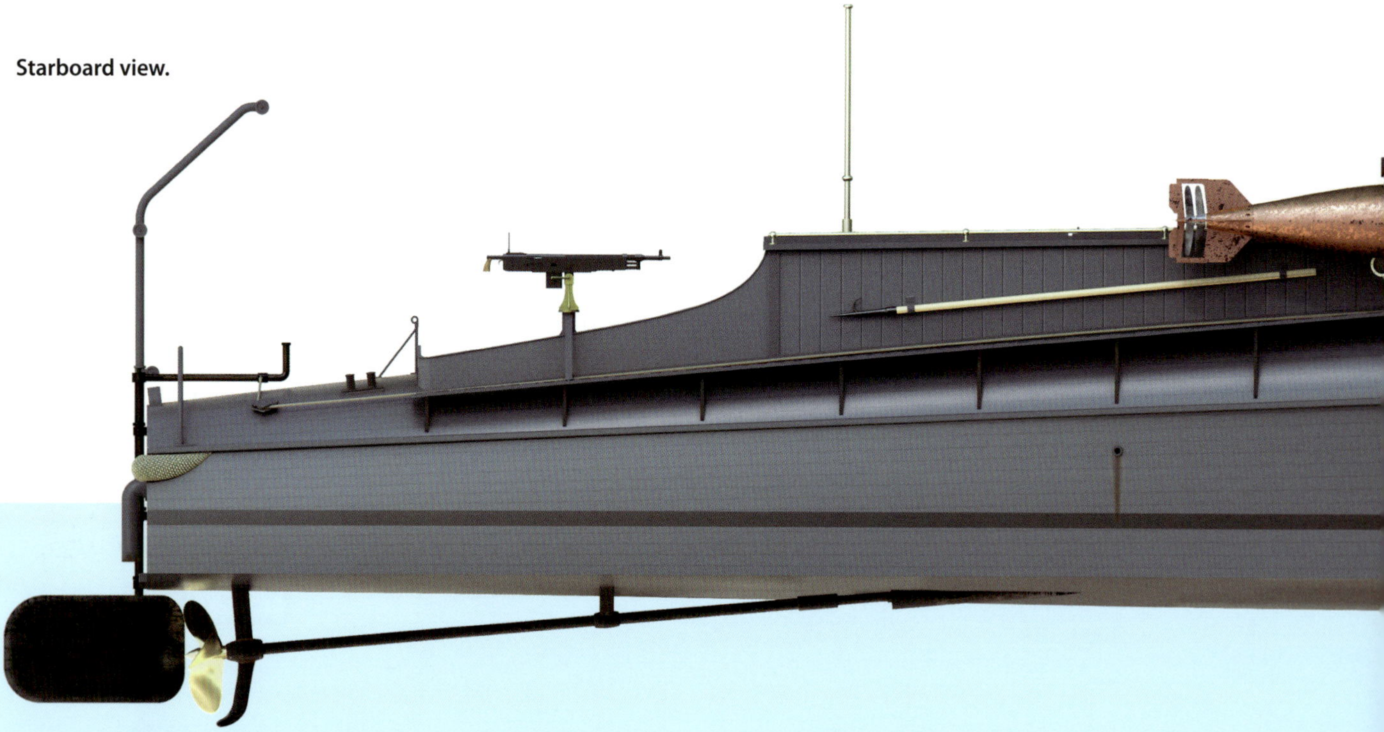

cutter started the attack, the "tongs" threw the torpedoes over both sides into the "ready" position with the help of simple articulated (hinged) levers. The torpedoes were hanging over the water. At the moment of the shot, the "claws" opened, allowing the torpedo to fall into the water; while turning on its engine. The torpedo was gaining momentum by itself, following the cutter's course. Such a system was light, simple and allowed for favourable weight distribution on light torpedo boats. It made it possible to carry out a torpedo salvo

MAS-21 in anti-submarine version with a 47 mm gun [WLB Stuttgart]

Italian torpedo boat OS-18, Spezia, 1916 [WLB Stuttgart]

Starboard view. Torpedoes in combat position.

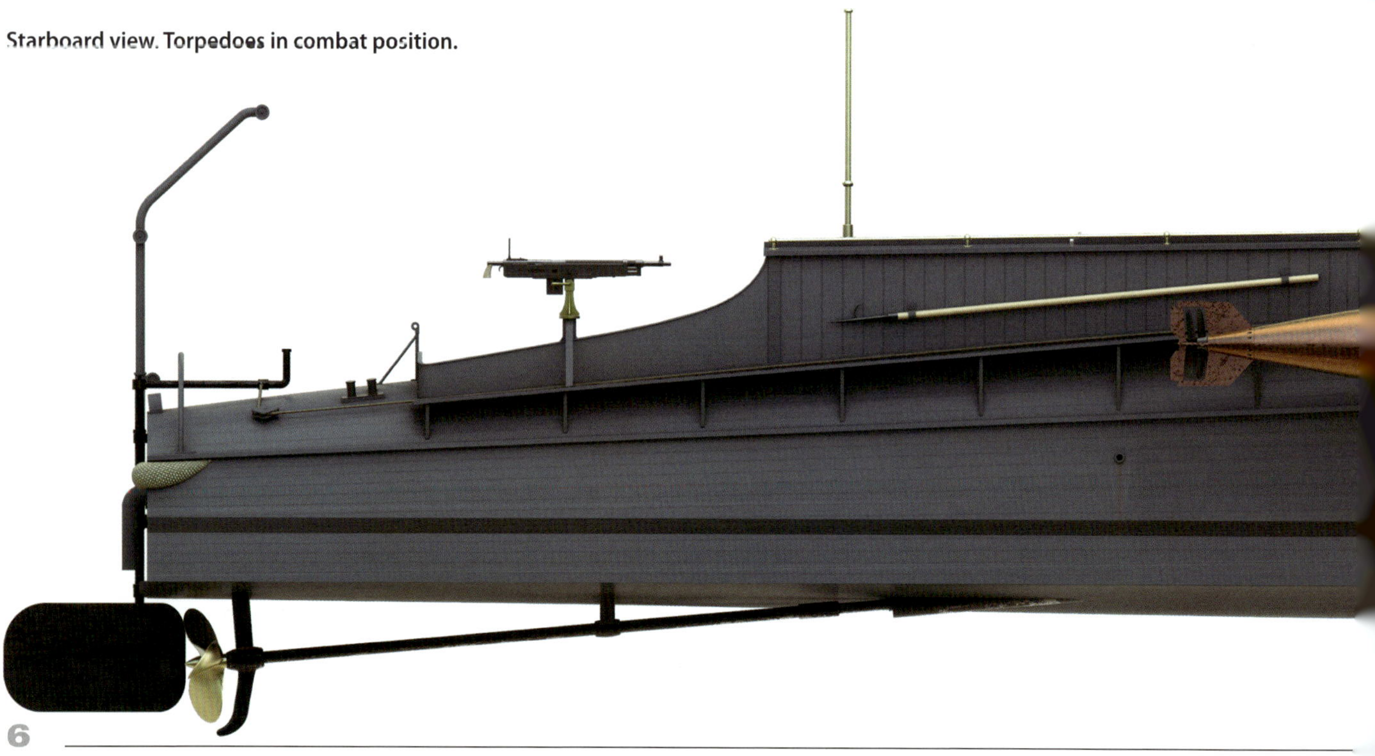

at a very low speed, and even when the cutter was standing still. The way the torpedoes were dropped by side also had its drawbacks. Even the slightest delay in starting the torpedo engine could lead to the fact that the firing of only one of the two torpedoes resulted in a significant inclination of the boat to the other side. Besides, in conditions of poor visibility it was impossible to attack the enemy at speeds exceeding the speed of the torpedo. The first to receive

Italian OS-15 torpedo boat [WLB Stuttgart]

General characteristics	
Displacement (tonnes)	– 12,5 Artillery version – 12,3 Torpedo version
Dimensions (m)	– Length – 16 – Beam – 2,61 – Draught – 1,2
Propusion	– 2x six cylinder Isotta-Fraschini L56 petrol engines producing 450 hp – 2x additional 10 hp Rognini & Balbo electric motors to keep the boats silent below 4 knots (7.4 km/h)
Speed (knots)	– full ahead – 24 – on electric motors – 4
Armament	– 2x 450 mm torpedoes – 2x 6.5 mm Colt-Browning M1895/14 – 47/40 H 1901 – QF 3-pounder Hotchkiss (Motor Gun Boat configuration) – 4x 37.5 kg depth charges – 4x Bollo mines (some boats)
Endurance	160 at 23 knots 160–200 nautical miles at top speeds (22–25 knots) or 20 nautical miles entirely running silent at 4 knots
Crew	8

Top view.

Top view. Torpedoes in combat position.

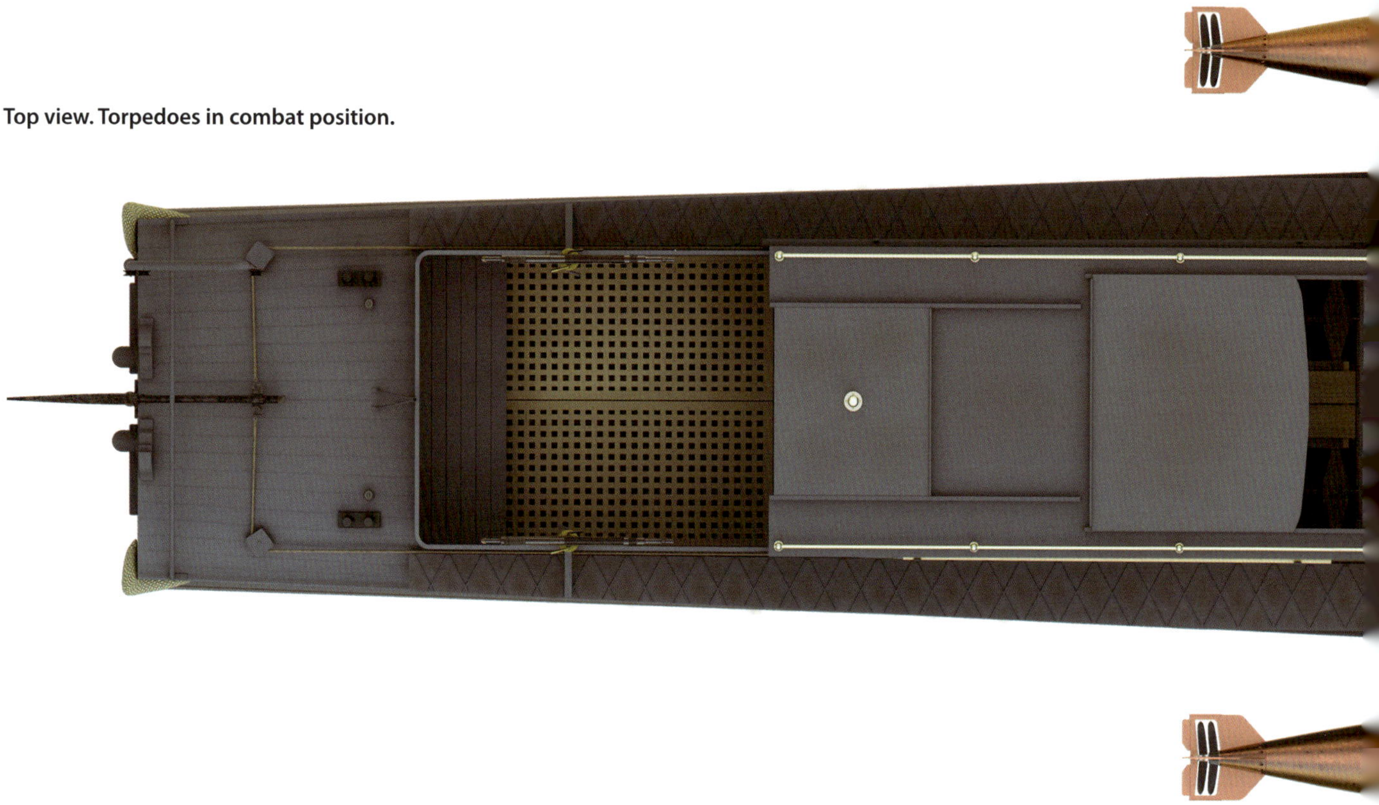

Another shot of MAS-15 [public domain]

this system was the MAS-5 and MAS-7 (rebuilt from anti-submarine cutters).

Another problem faced by engineer Bisio was the loud noise of working aircraft engines, which revealed the presence of cutters. All attempts to silence them by using various types of jammers have been unsuccessful. An effective solution to the noise problem was the use of additional electric motors and batteries. Rognin-Balbo's electro-motors from Milan had 5 HP of power. Two such motors (280 rpm), working on one shaft, were installed on each cutter. They were powered by a 25-element battery. The solution was not ideal, because the weight of the engines and batteries was 1.5 tons. So the displacement increased and the maximum speed decreased. The additional propulsion limited the already small space in these little boats. The limitation was the low speed – only four knots (maintained for five hours) and the short range – 12–20 nautical miles. In this situation, the cutters had to arrive at the scene with basic engines or were towed by torpedo boats. Then they turned on

the electric motors and quietly approached the target in conditions of low and poor visibility. One could hear the hum of these engines from a distance of only 50–100 meters. In water, with the use of hydrophones, audibility ranged from 300 to 500 meters. It was only in the last phase of the attack that they restarted the gasoline engines and attacked their victim at maximum speed, then departed from the scene at full speed.

Positive results of the tests of electric motors on the MAS-20 allowed for the decision to install them (at the turn of 1916/1917) on subsequent units: MAS-9, MAS-10, MAS-12–MAS-15, MAS-18, MAS-20–MAS-22. The additional electric drive in combination with the underwater exhaust of exhaust gases from internal combustion engines turned out to be quite effective. On the night of September 6–7, 1916, the MAS-1 and MAS-2 sank the Austro-Hungarian steamship "Lokrum" (924BRT) in Durazzo (now Albanian Durres). It was the first success of motor torpedo boats in history. This success encouraged the command of the Italian fleet to retool a few more cutters. The 47 mm gun was replaced with two torpedoes of the caliber of 450 mm of the side drop.

The small size of the cutters did not allow the installation of large 533 mm torpedoes. The 450 mm ones limited the combat capabilities of these units. Type A-68 torpedoes (model 1905) had a warhead containing only 45 kg of explosives. The newer model of the A-110 steam-gas torpedo (model 1913) already had a warhead containing 110 kg of explosive material. Nevertheless, the Italians, in a few cases, managed to sink large and armoured enemy ships with these torpedoes. Italian specialists constantly improved their "product". Engineers from Brindisi developed a new type of torpedo launcher. At the beginning of 1917, six cutters (MAS-9, 13, 14, 15, 18, 20, 21, 22) received new launchers. In the same year, the boats with additional electric motors: MAS-9, 13 and 15 were rebuilt in such a way that they could, if necessary, put up four "Bollo" mines.

The combat capabilities of the MAS' (like any other ship) could only be verified by naval warfare. Soon such an opportunity arose.

Bow view.

Bow view. Torpedoes in combat position.

Stern view.

Stern view. Torpedoes in combat position.

Bow part of the torpedo motor boat.

Port view of the hull mid and 450 mm torpedoes in "a telaio" type launchers.

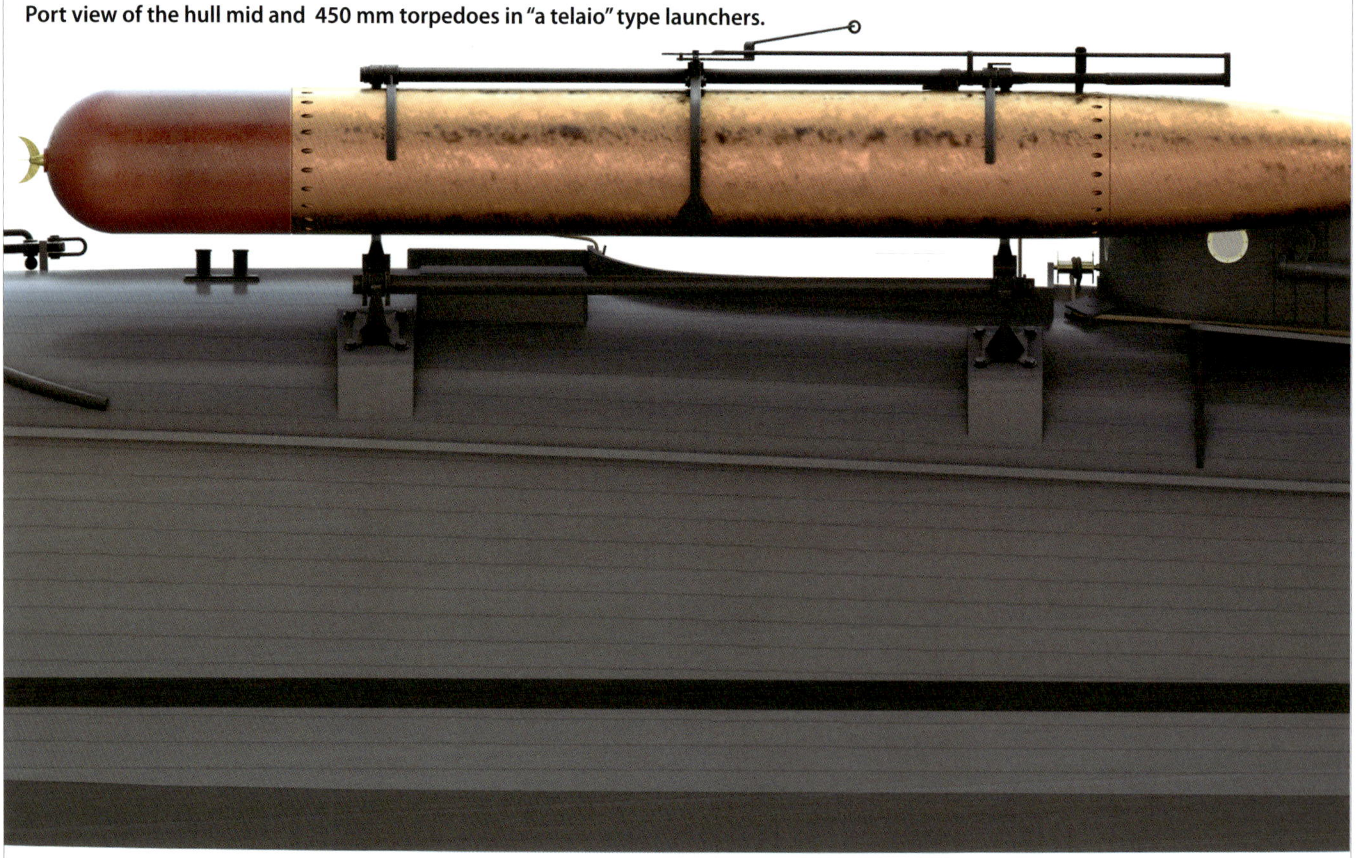

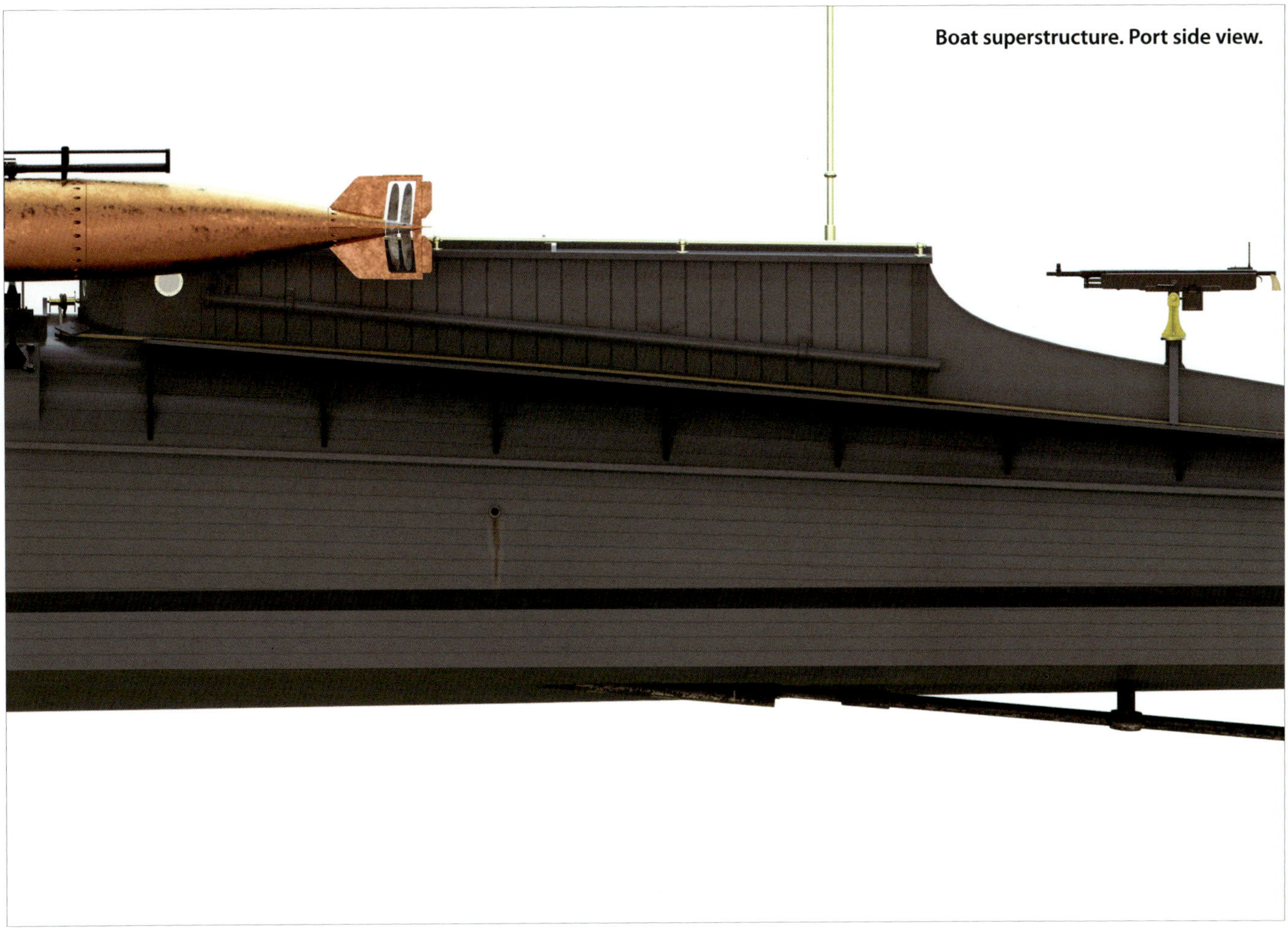

Boat superstructure. Port side view.

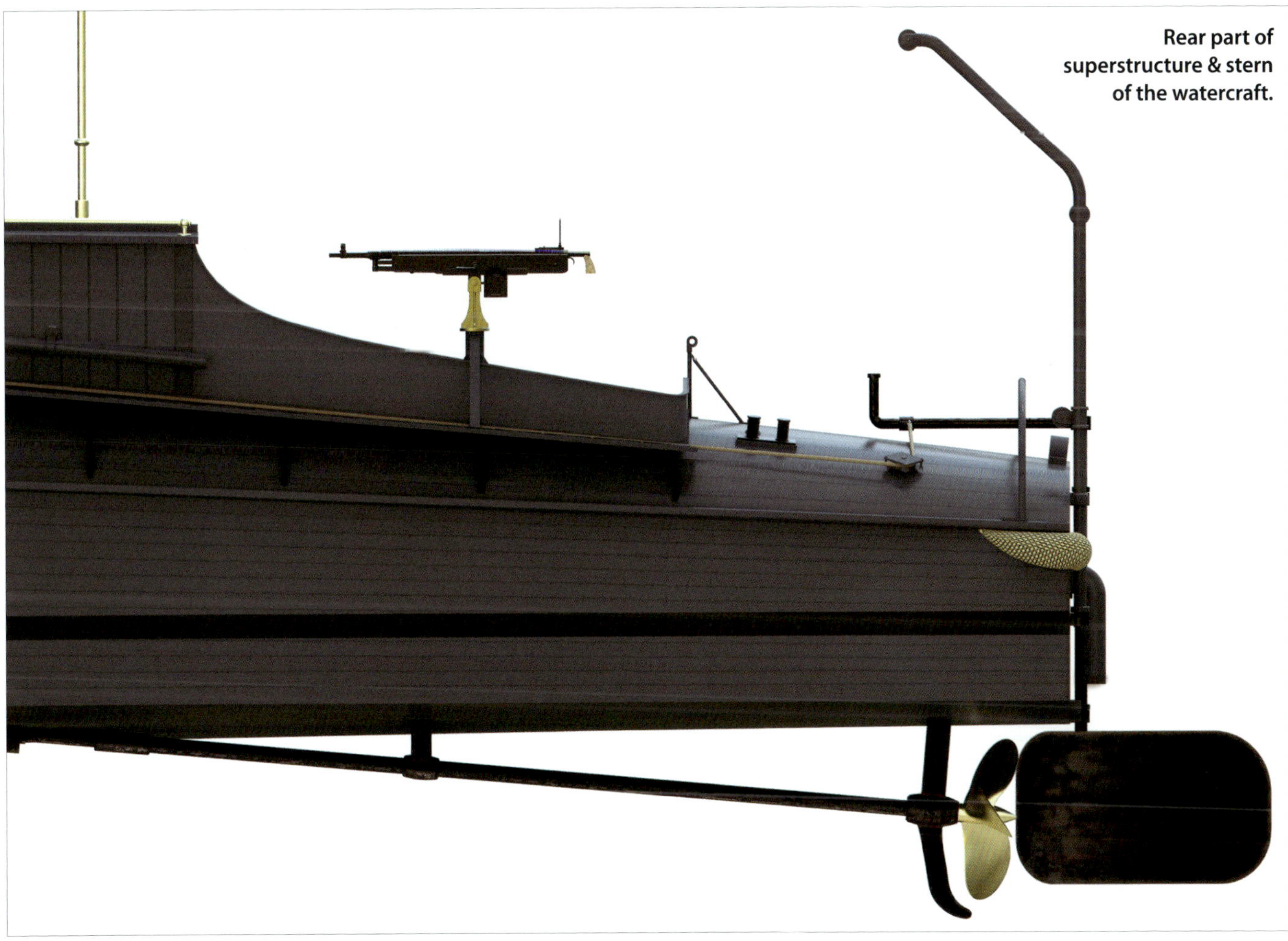

Rear part of superstructure & stern of the watercraft.

General views of the MAS-15.

M.A.S.15

Starboard view of the bow.

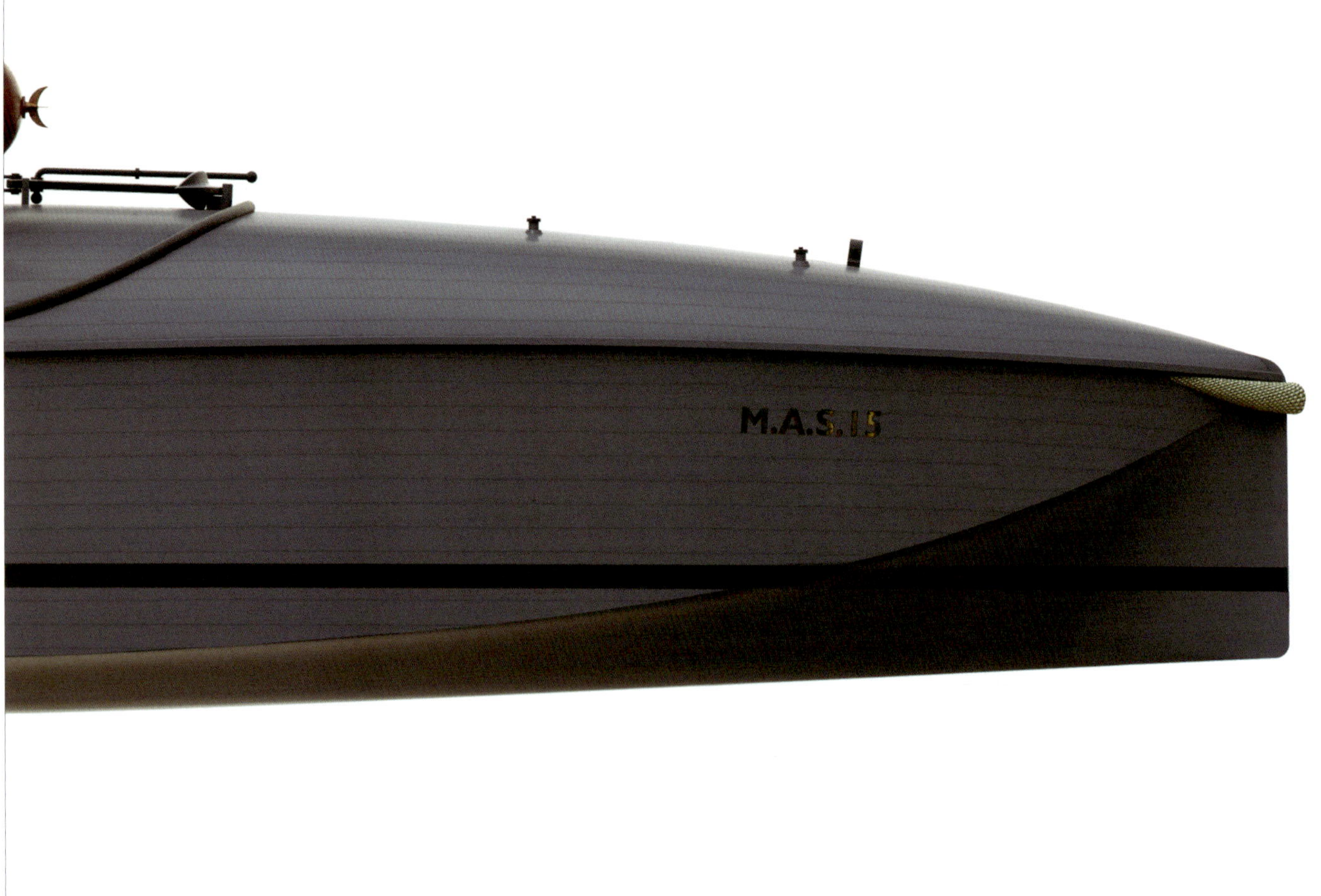

Mid hull & the right torpedo launcher. Starboard view.

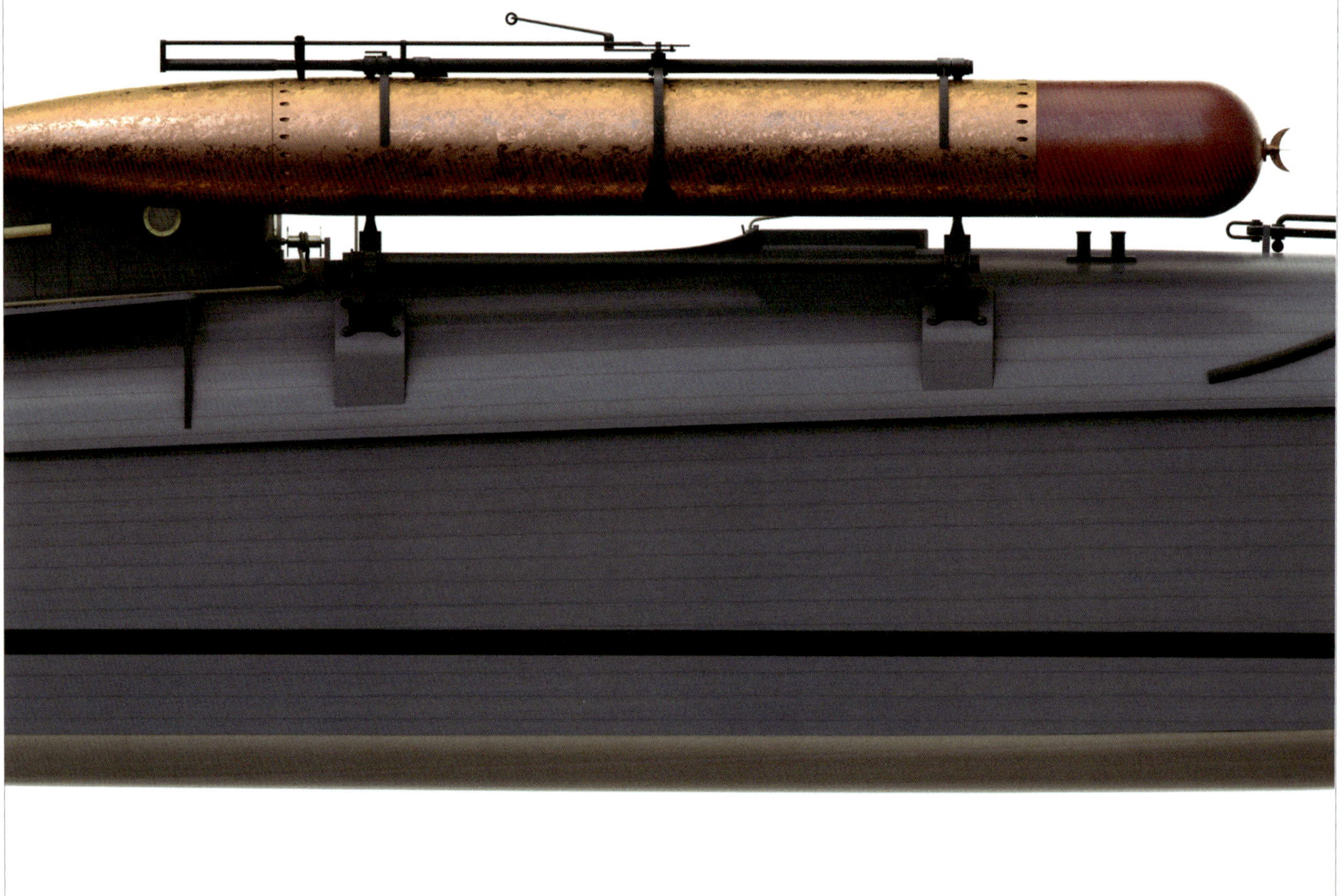

Starboard view of superstructure middle part.

Starboard view of the stern.

Top view of the bow with four fillers and anchor.

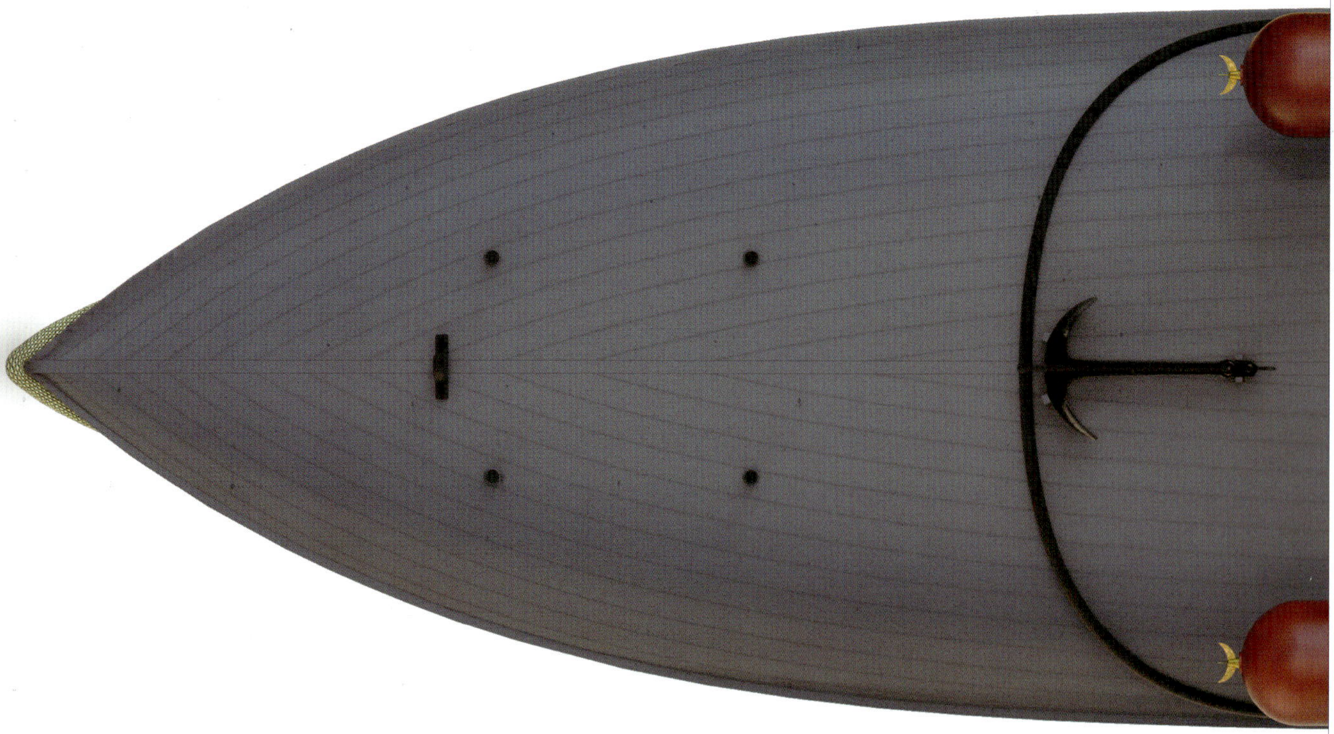

Top view of the middle part of the hull. Torpedo director is visible on the front of the superstructure.

View of the middle and rear of the superstructure. Top view.

Stern of the water-craft. Top view.

Rear of the left torpedo launcher.

Front pivot support of the left torpedo launcher.

Rear pivot support of the left torpedo launcher.

Technical section.

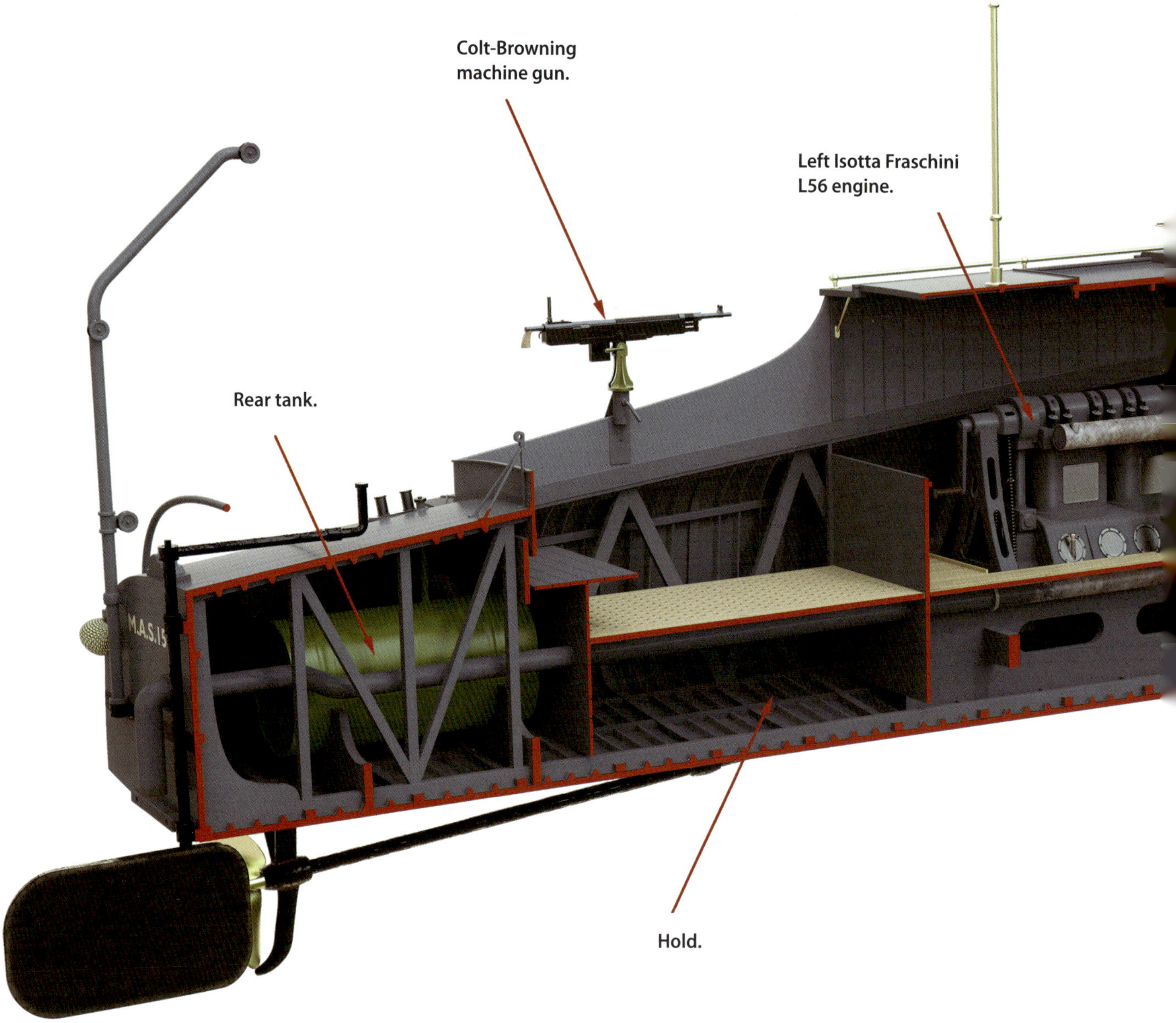

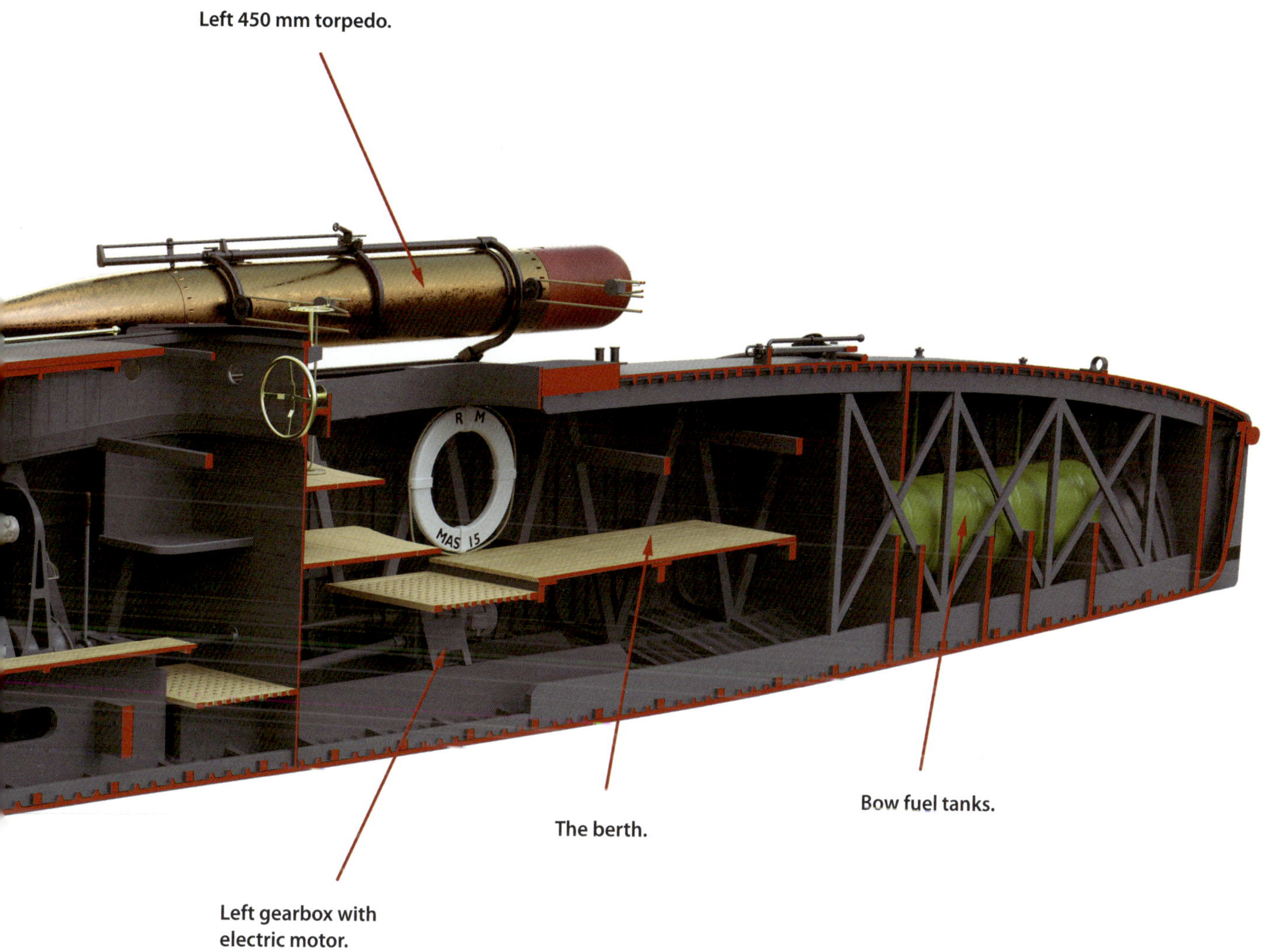
Left 450 mm torpedo.
R M
MAS 15
The berth.
Bow fuel tanks.
Left gearbox with
electric motor.

A bird's eye port bow view of the superstructure.

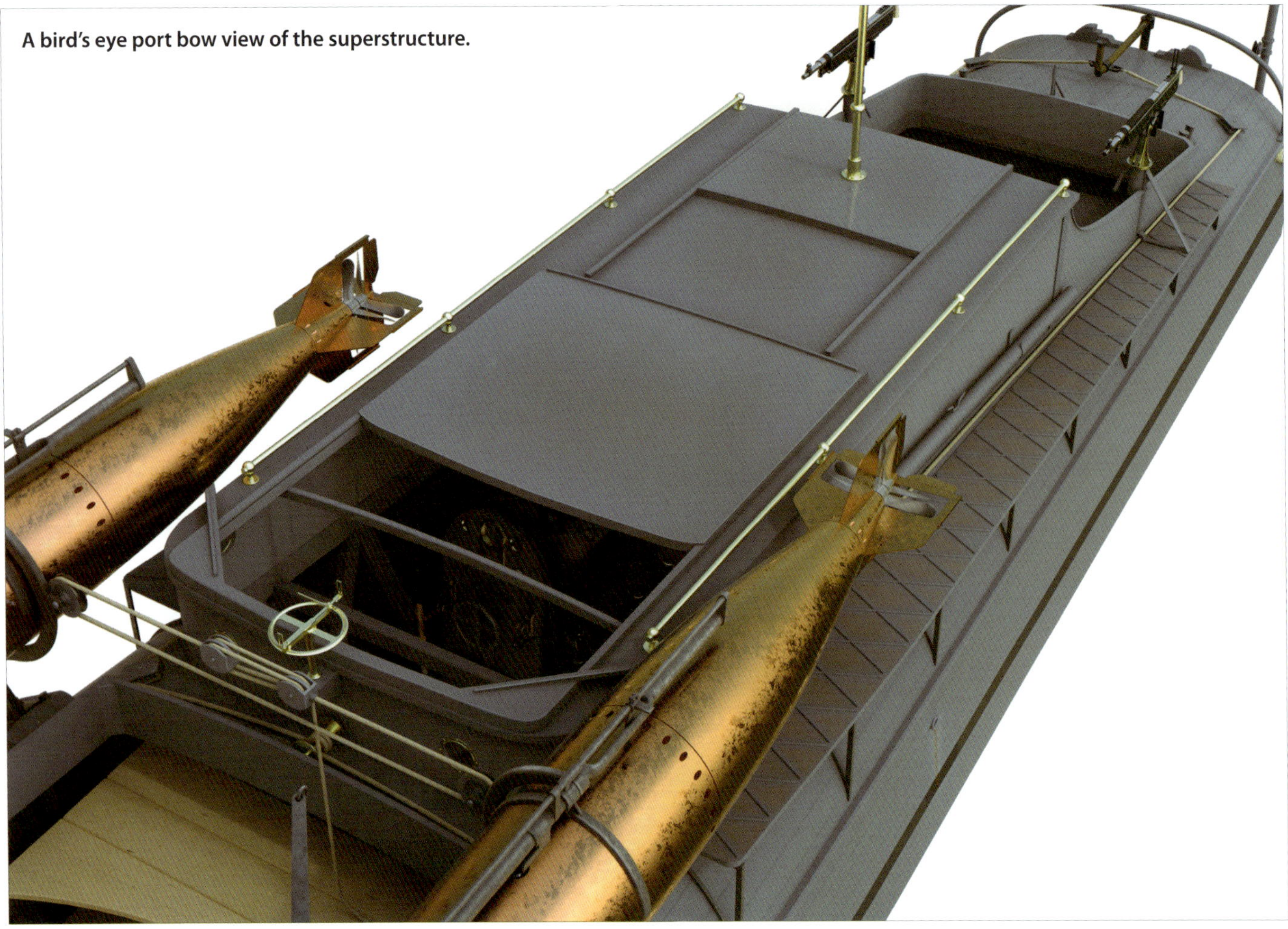

The same position. The roof of the superstructure is not shown.

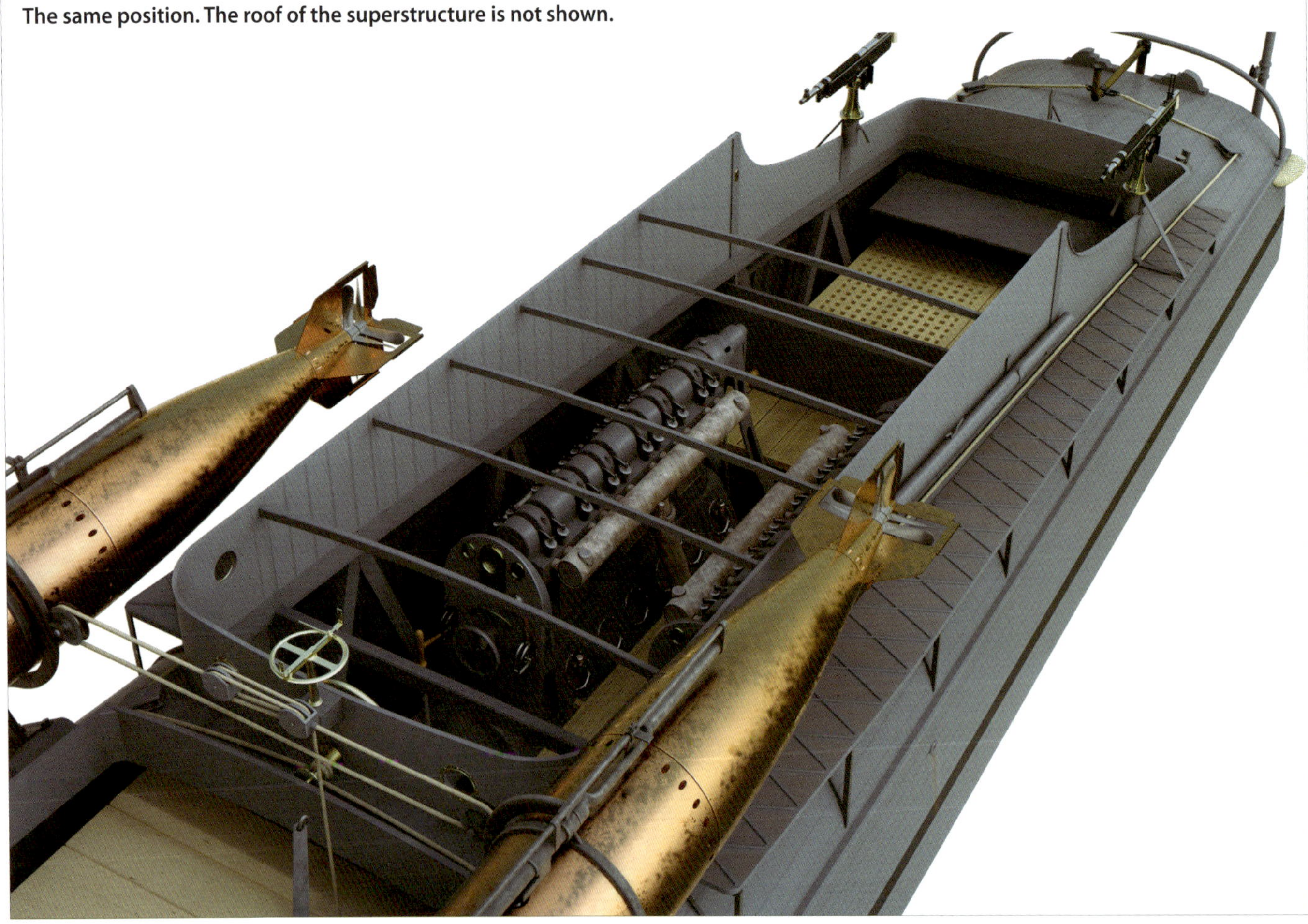

The superstructure. Astern view from above.

The same view but the roof of the superstructure is not shown.

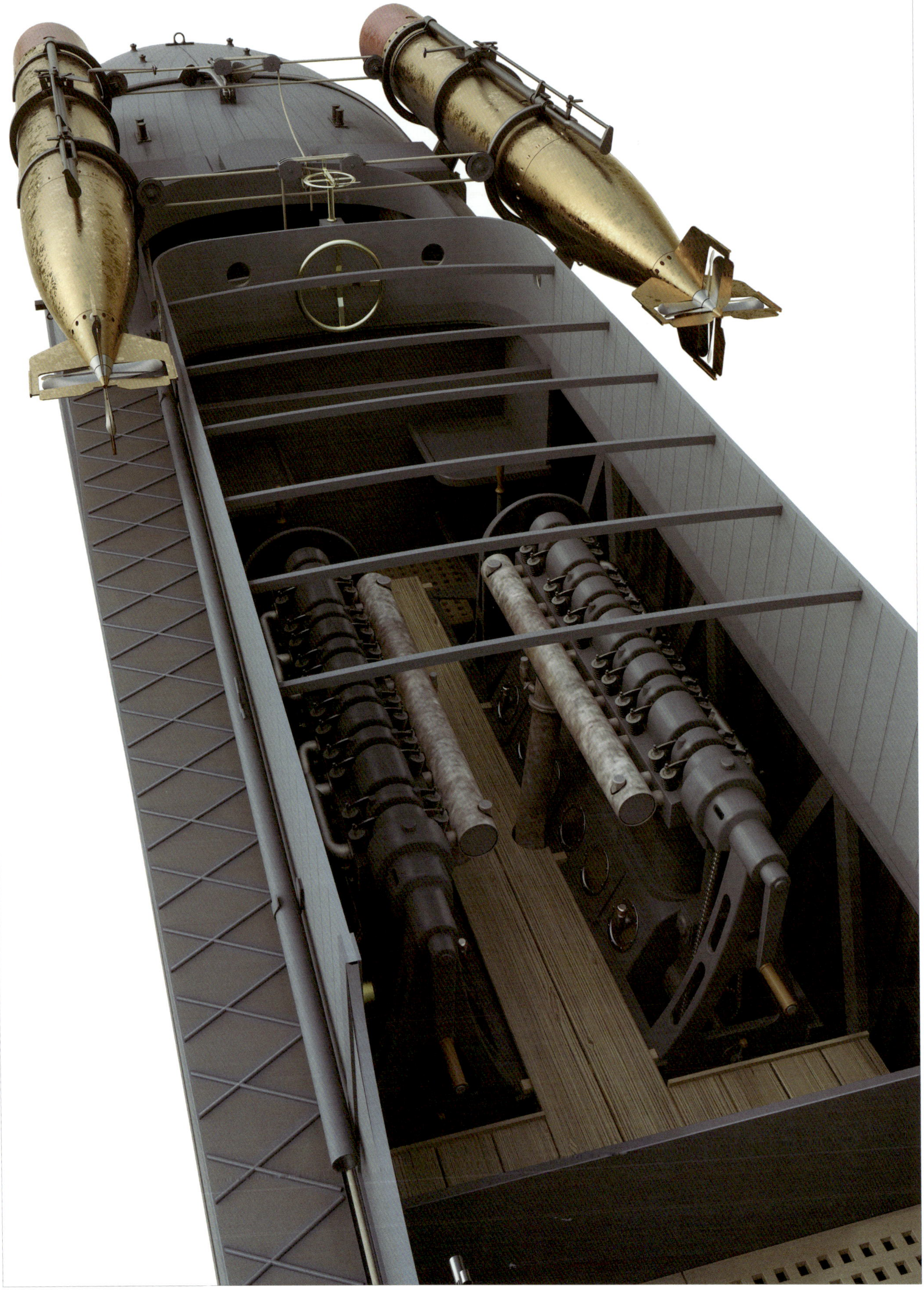

The rear of the superstructure with a machine gun platform. Astern view.

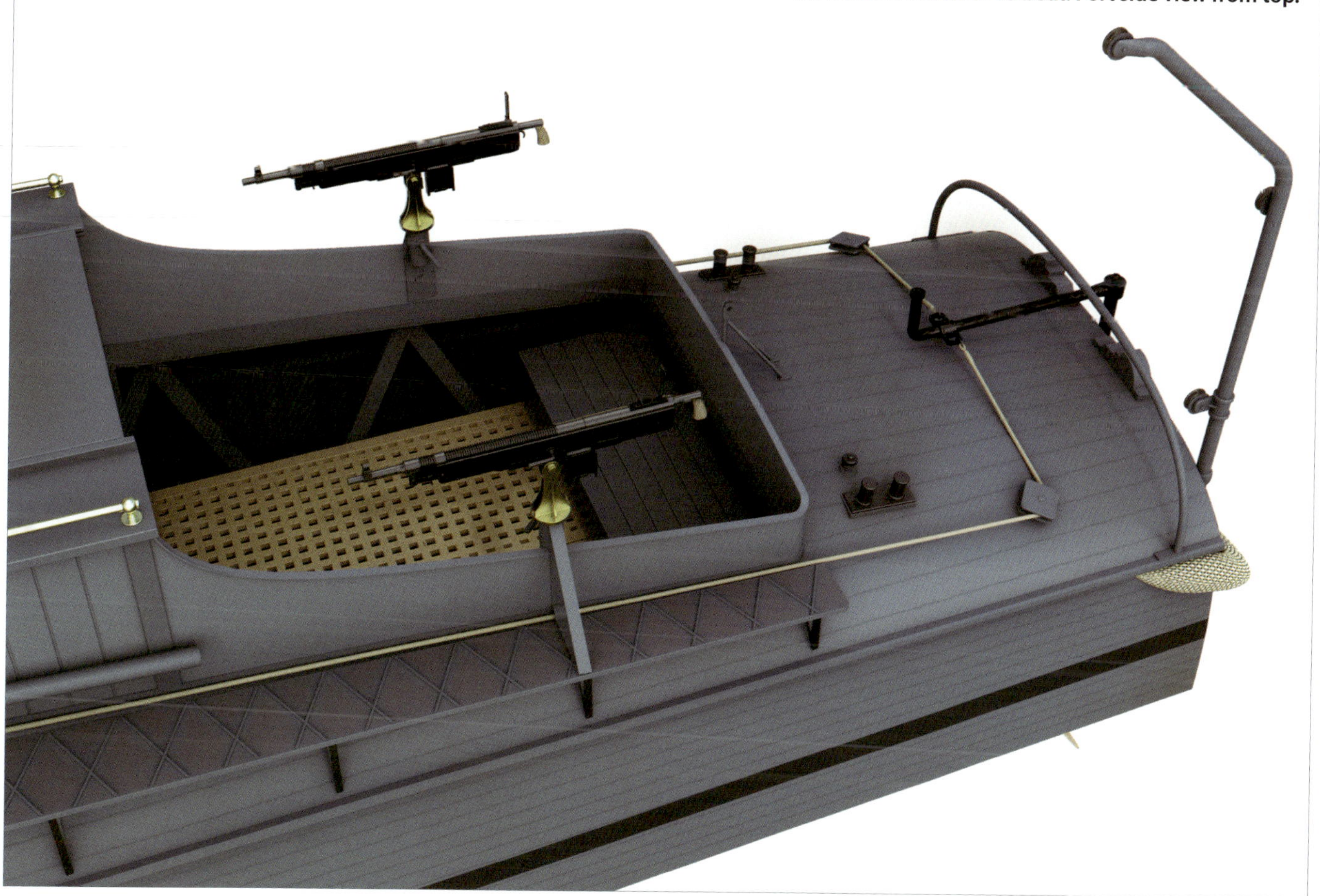

The stern of the MAS-15 boat. Port side view from top.

The stern of the motor torpedo boat.

The stern of the water-craft. View from bottom.

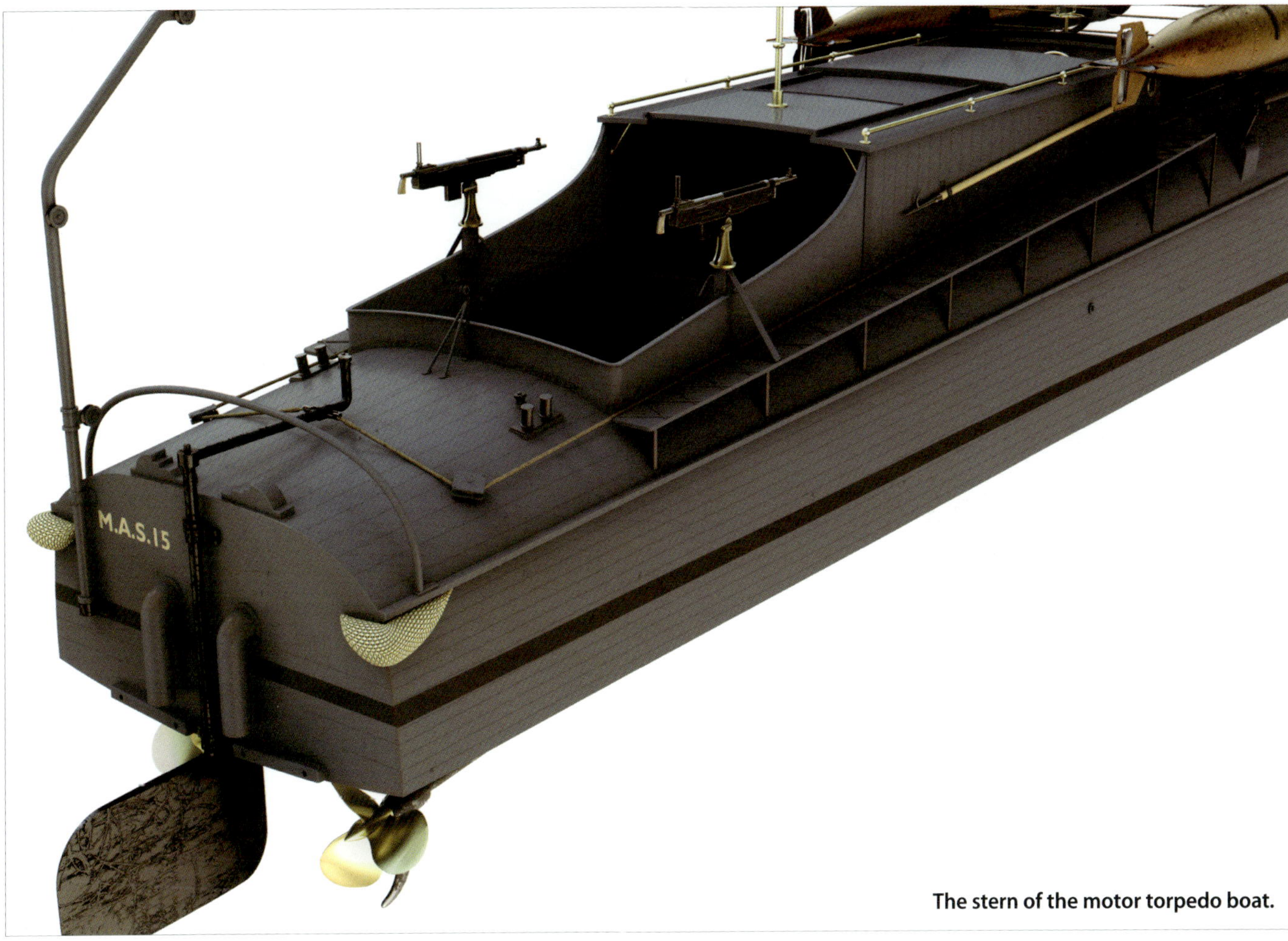

The stern of the motor torpedo boat.

Colt-Browning machine gun.

Isotta Fraschini L56 engine. Left rear view.

Isotta Fraschini L56 engine. Right front view.

Engine control panel.

6.5 mm Colt-Browning machine gun. Right side.

Colt-Browning machine gun. Left side.

Left gearbox with electric motor.

The 45 cm torpedo.

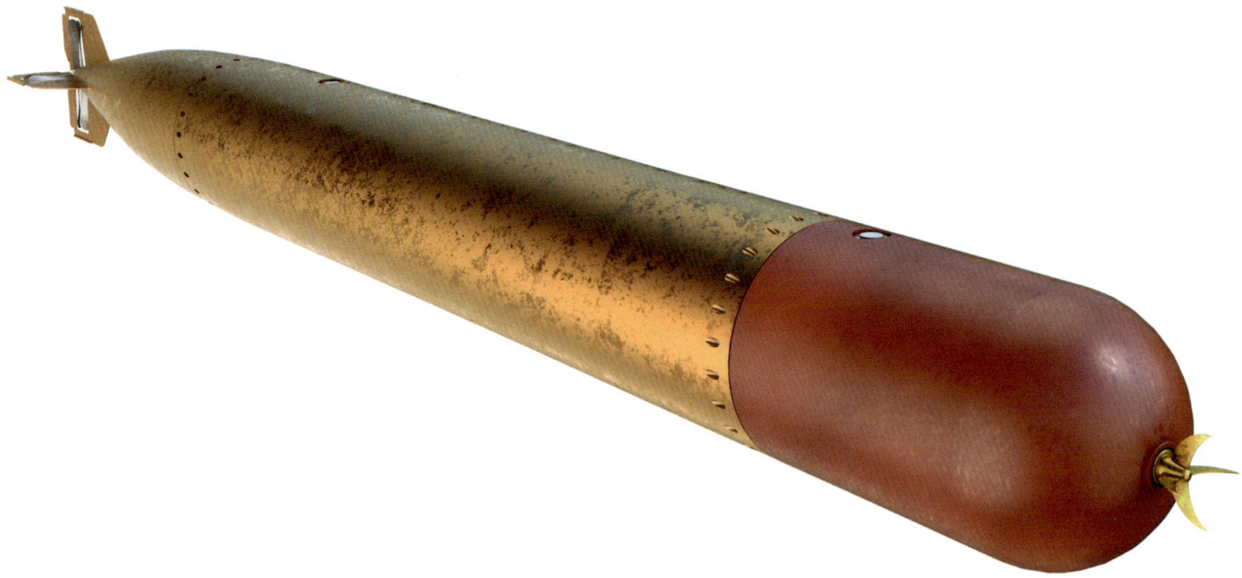

The tail section of the torpedo.

Fuse with knives to destroy anti-torpedo nets.

Wooden body structure.

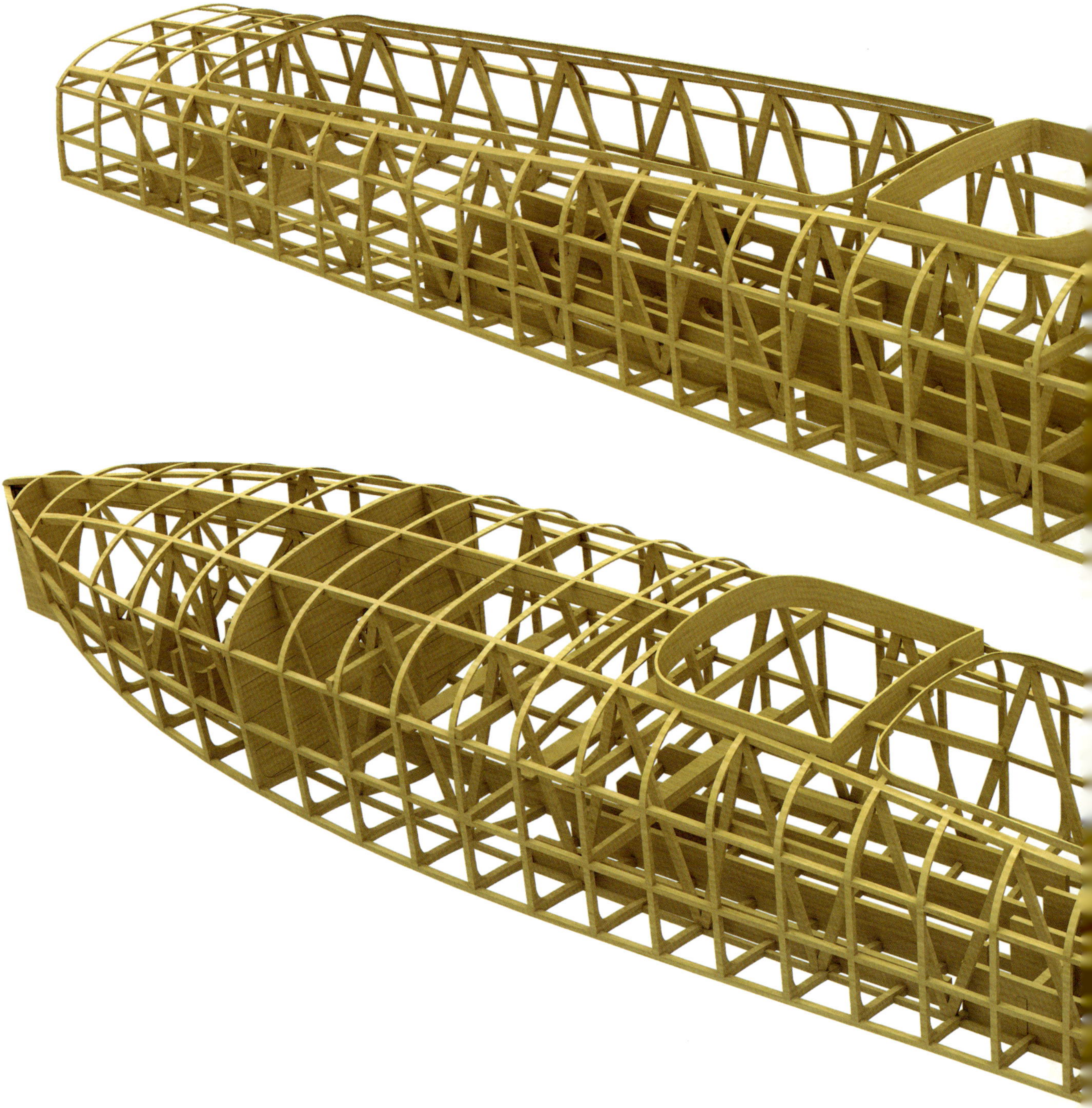

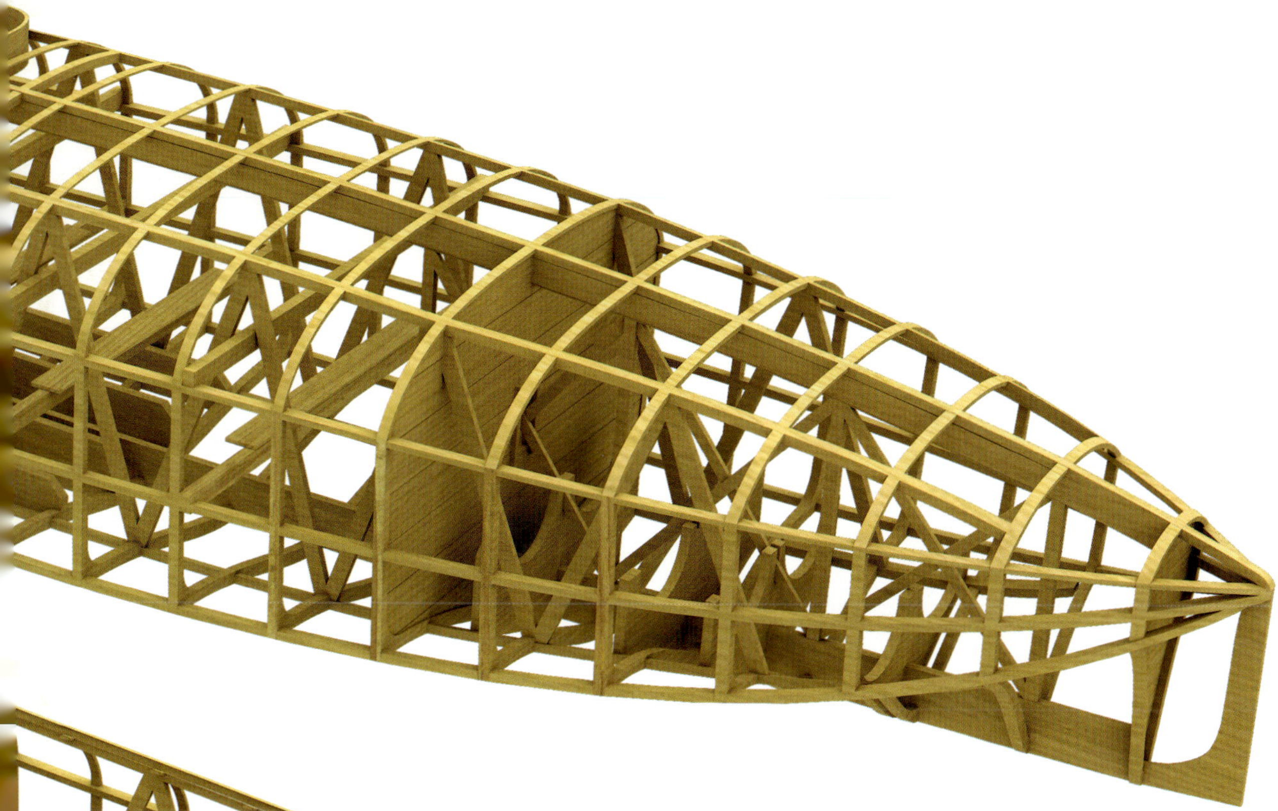

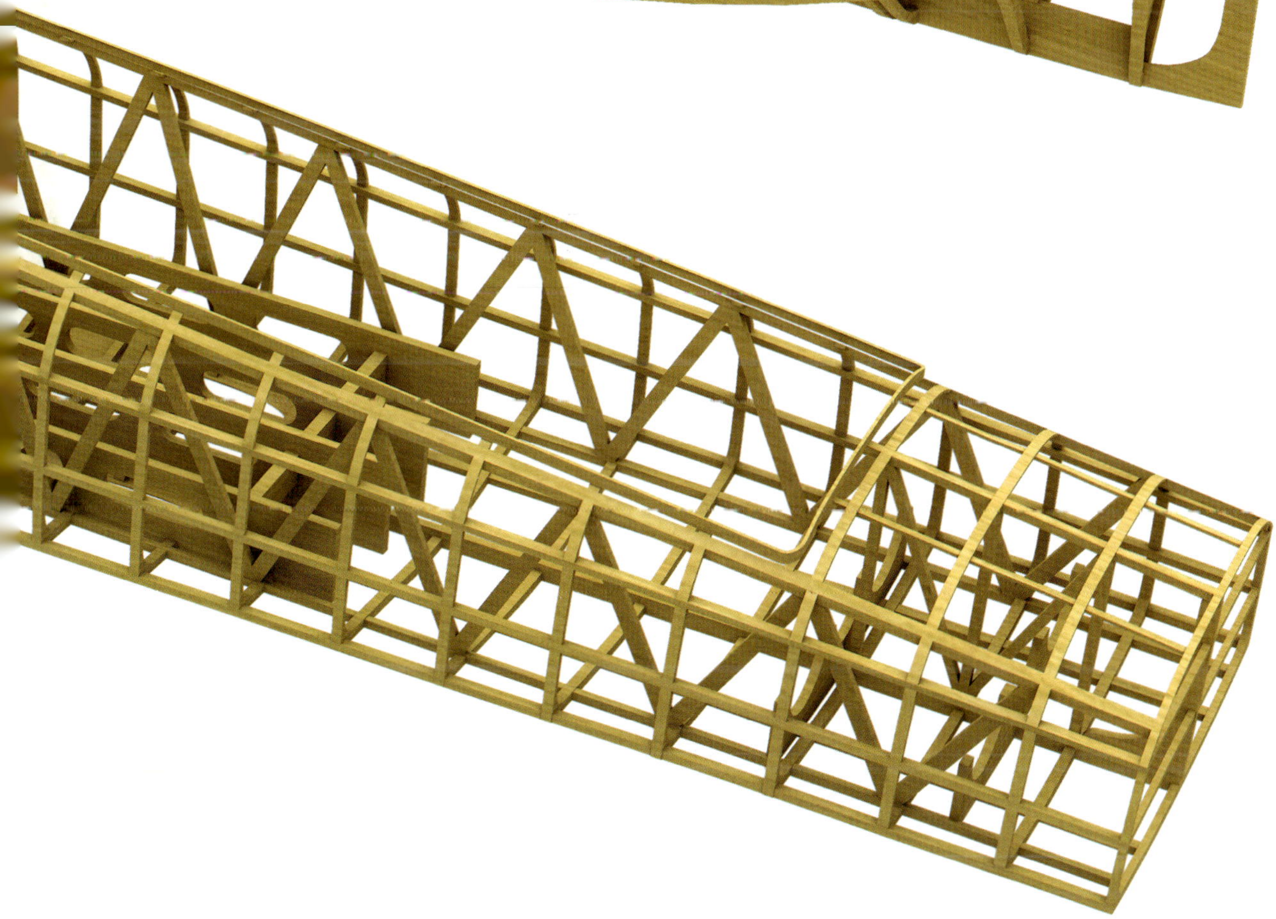

Wooden body structure. Stern view.

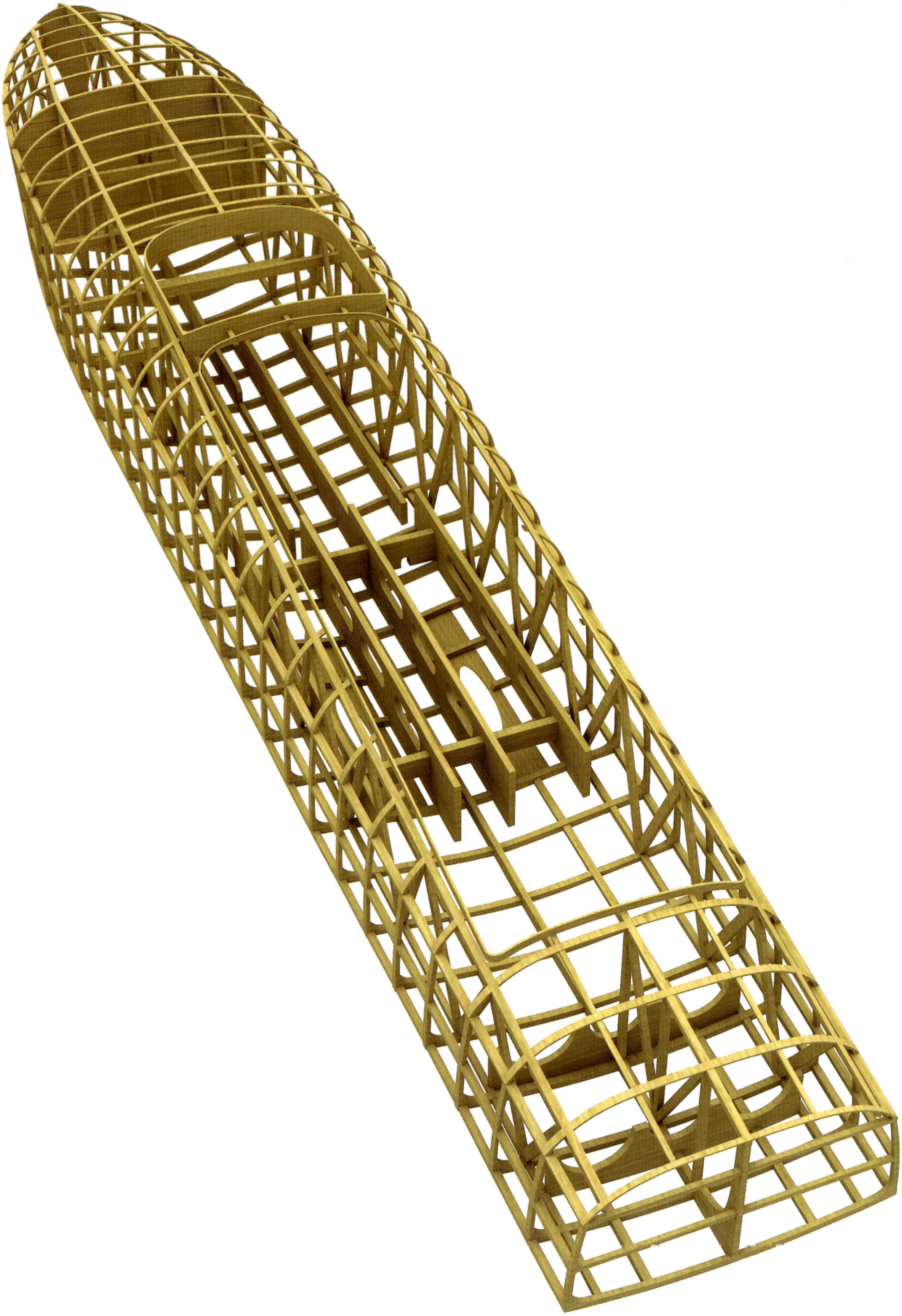

Wooden body structure. Bow view.

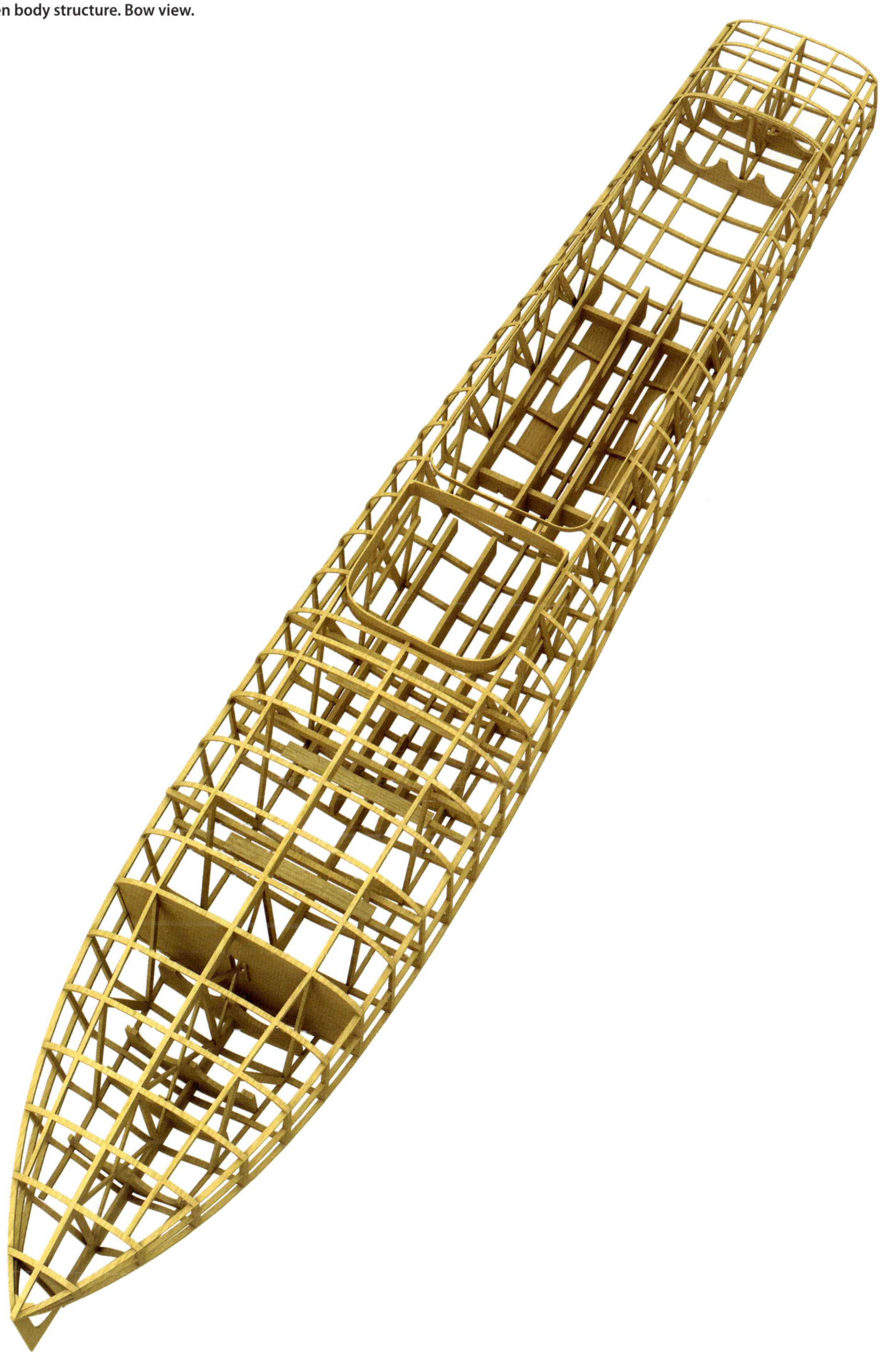

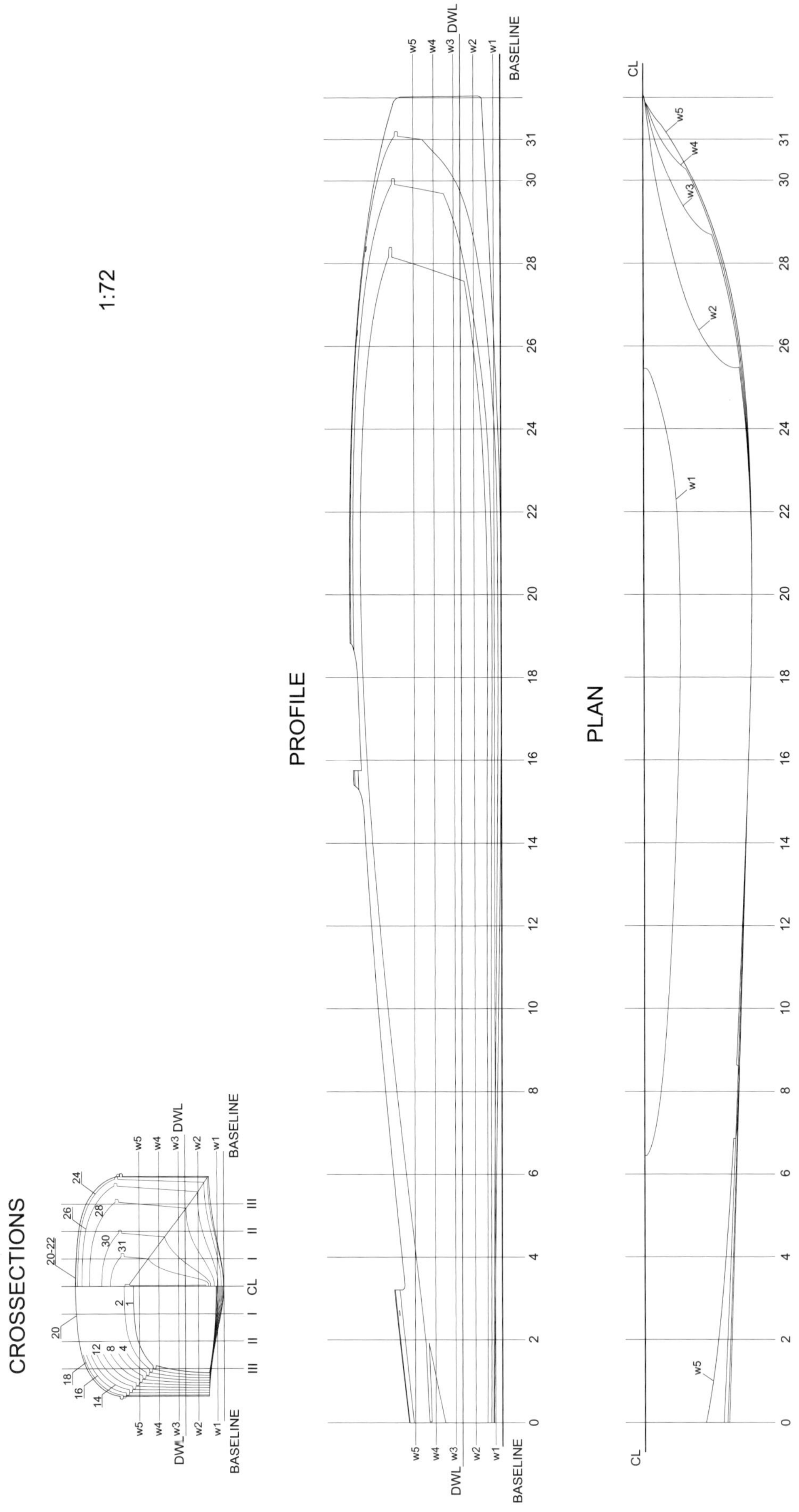
1:72
CROSSECTIONS
PROFILE
PLAN
BASELINE
DWL
w1
w2
w3
w4
w5
CL

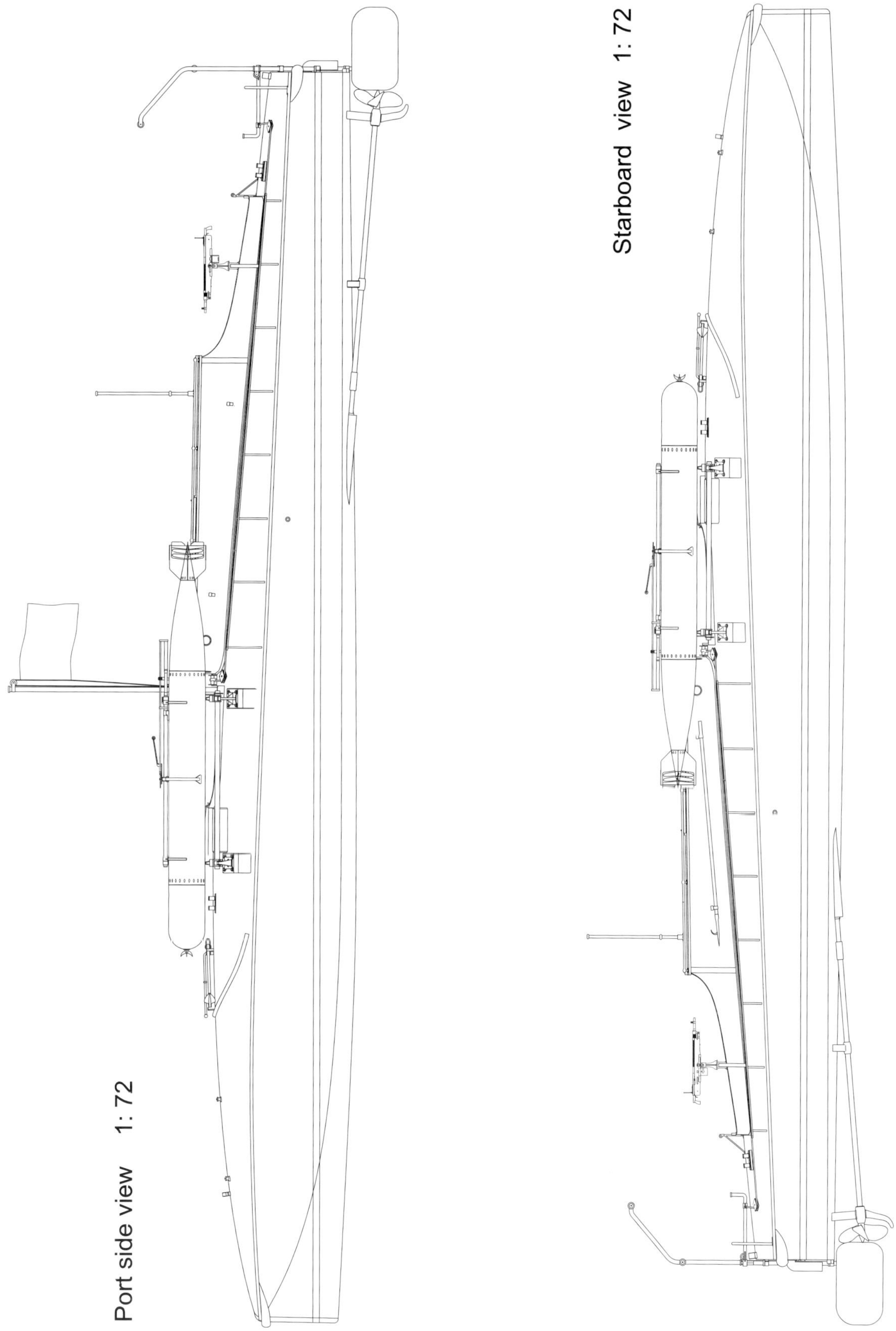

Port side view 1: 72

Starboard view 1: 72

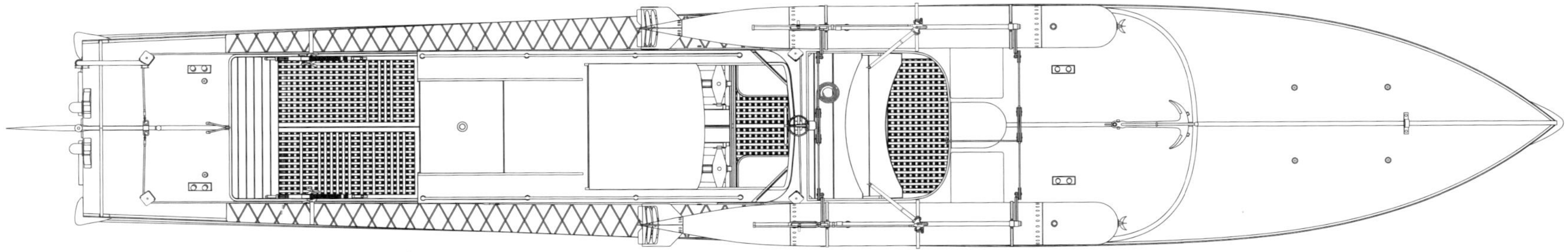

Top view. Torpedoes in the stowed position.

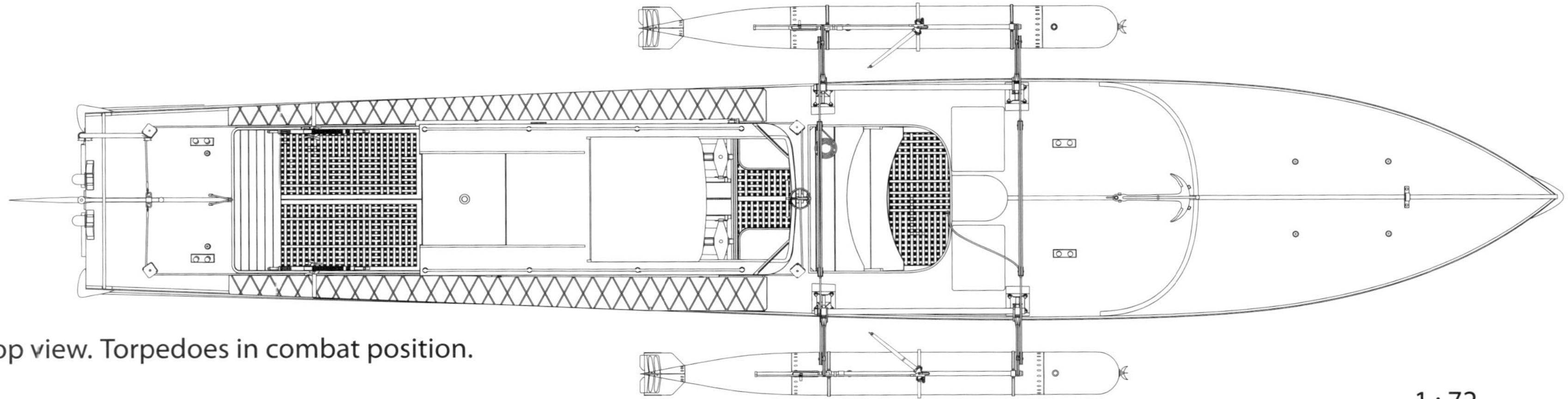

Top view. Torpedoes in combat position.

1 : 72

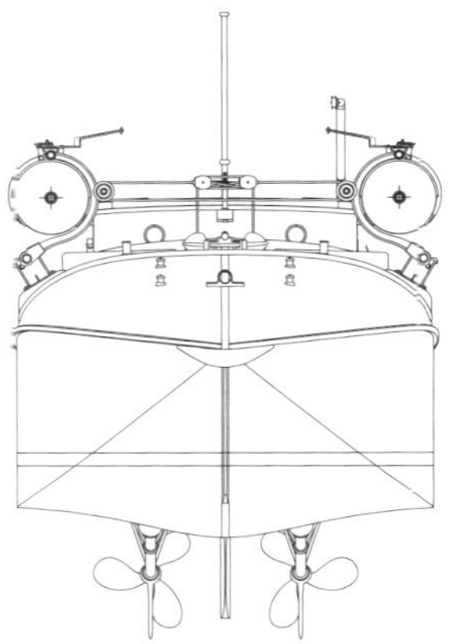

Bow view.

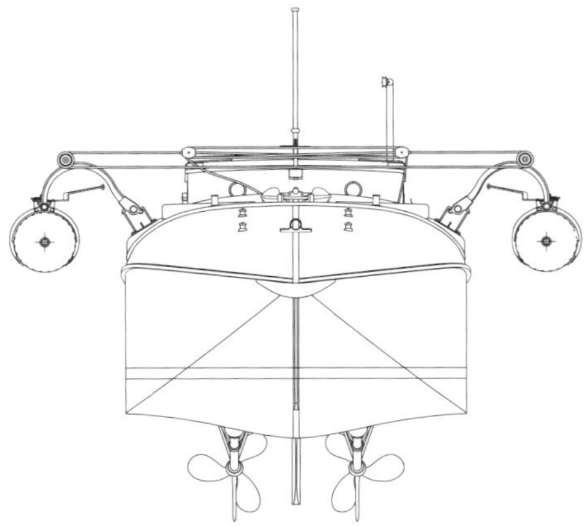

Bow view. Torpedoes in combat position.

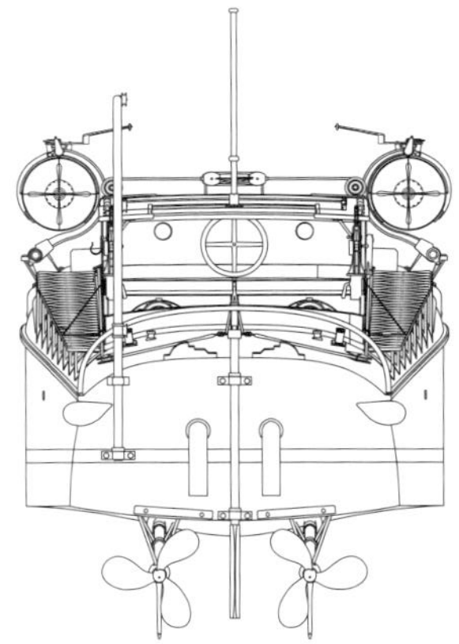

Stern view.

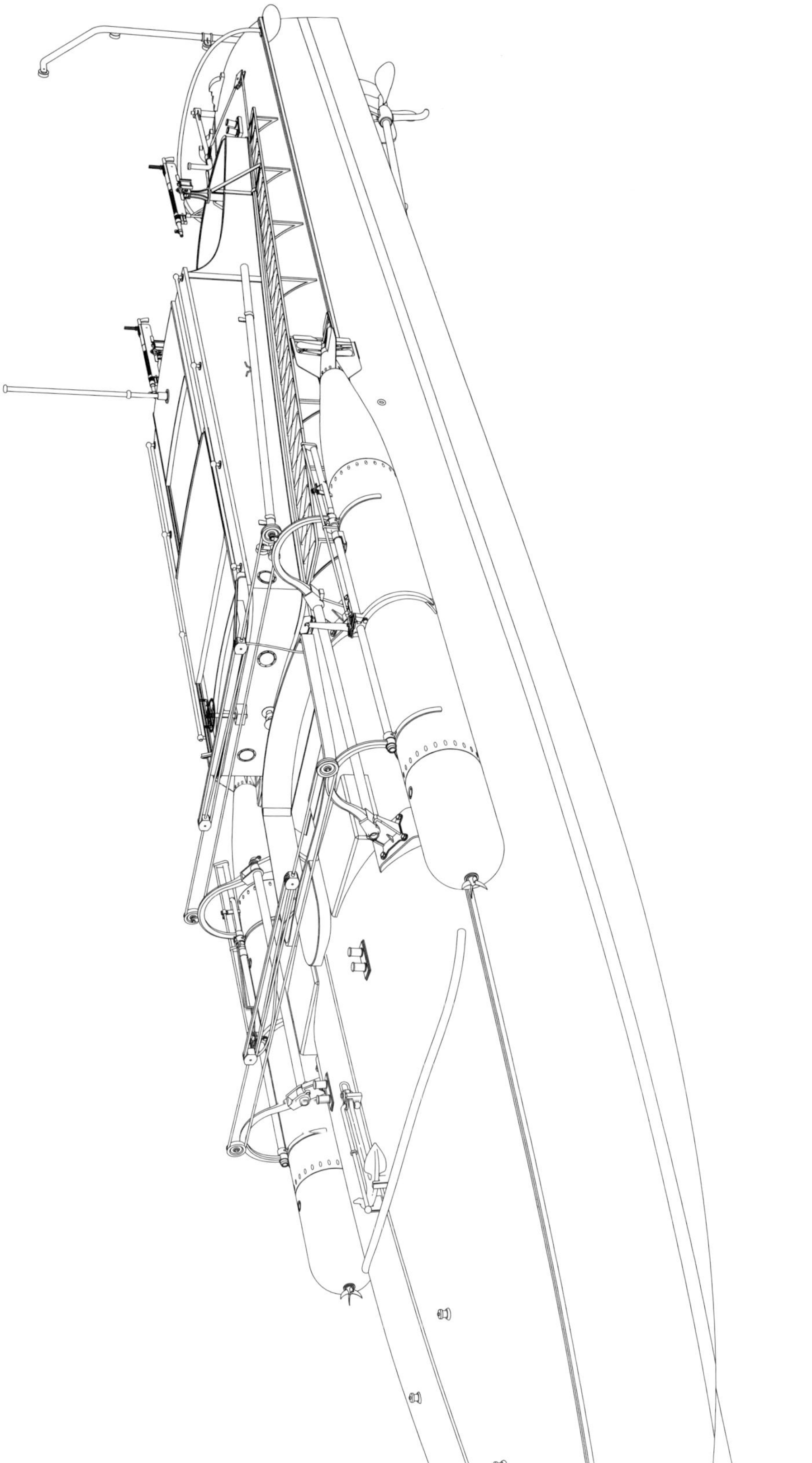

Bow port side view. Torpedoes in combat position.

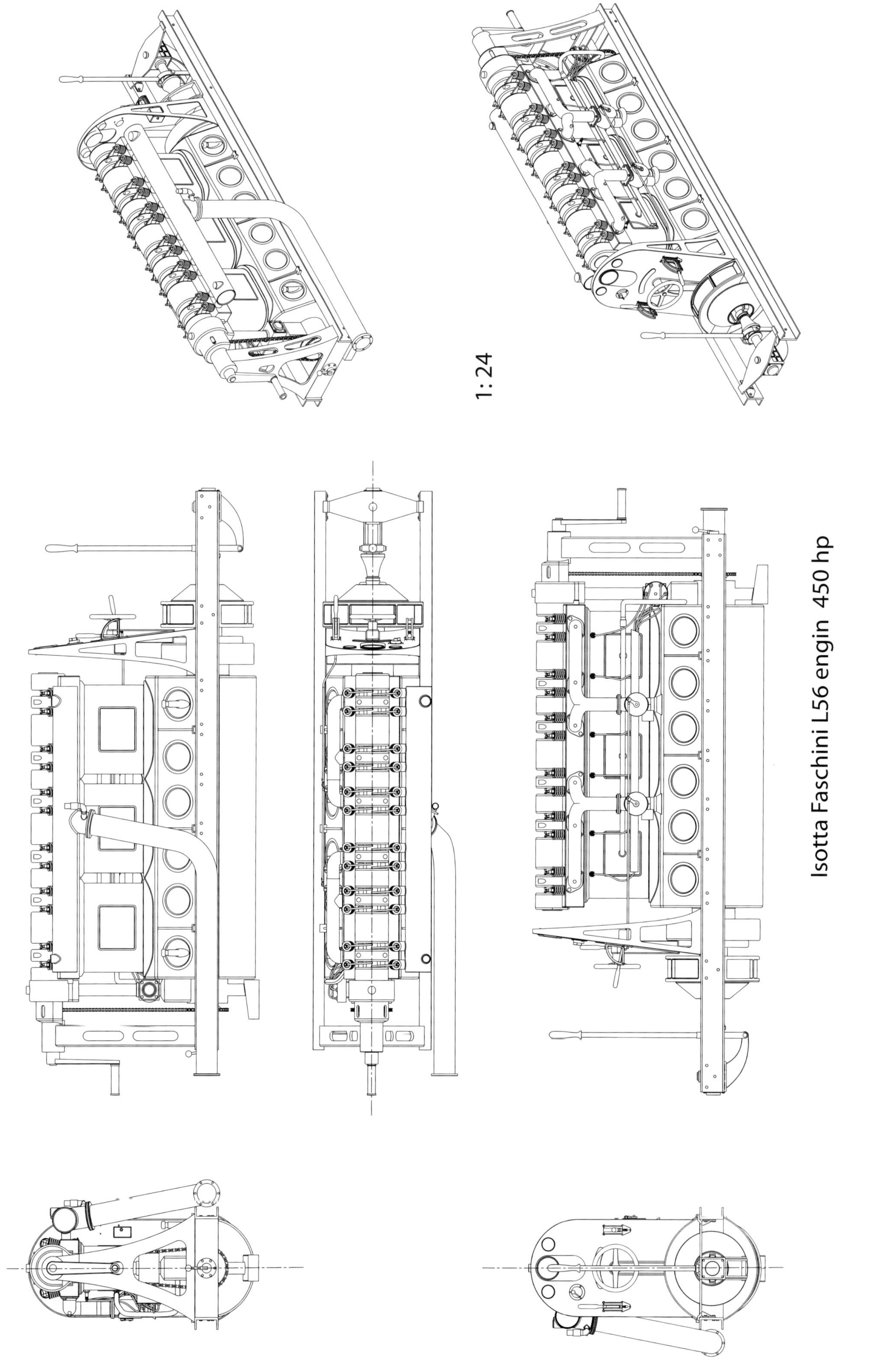
1: 24
Isotta Faschini L56 engin 450 hp

6.5 mm Colt-Browning machine gun (1895)

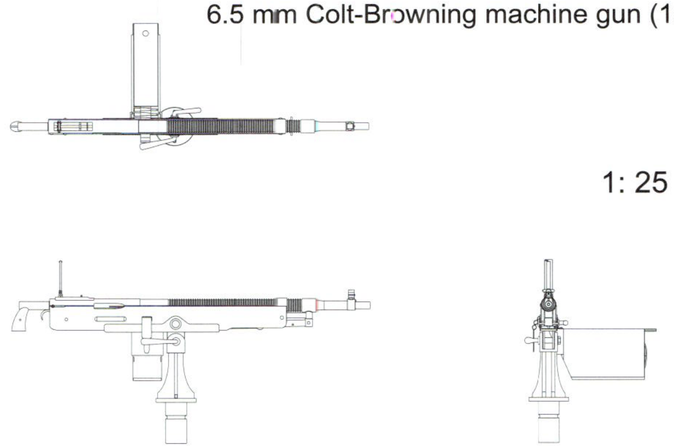

1: 25

Damage of the SMS "Szent Istvan" battleship as a result of the torpedo attack of the MAS-15 motor boat

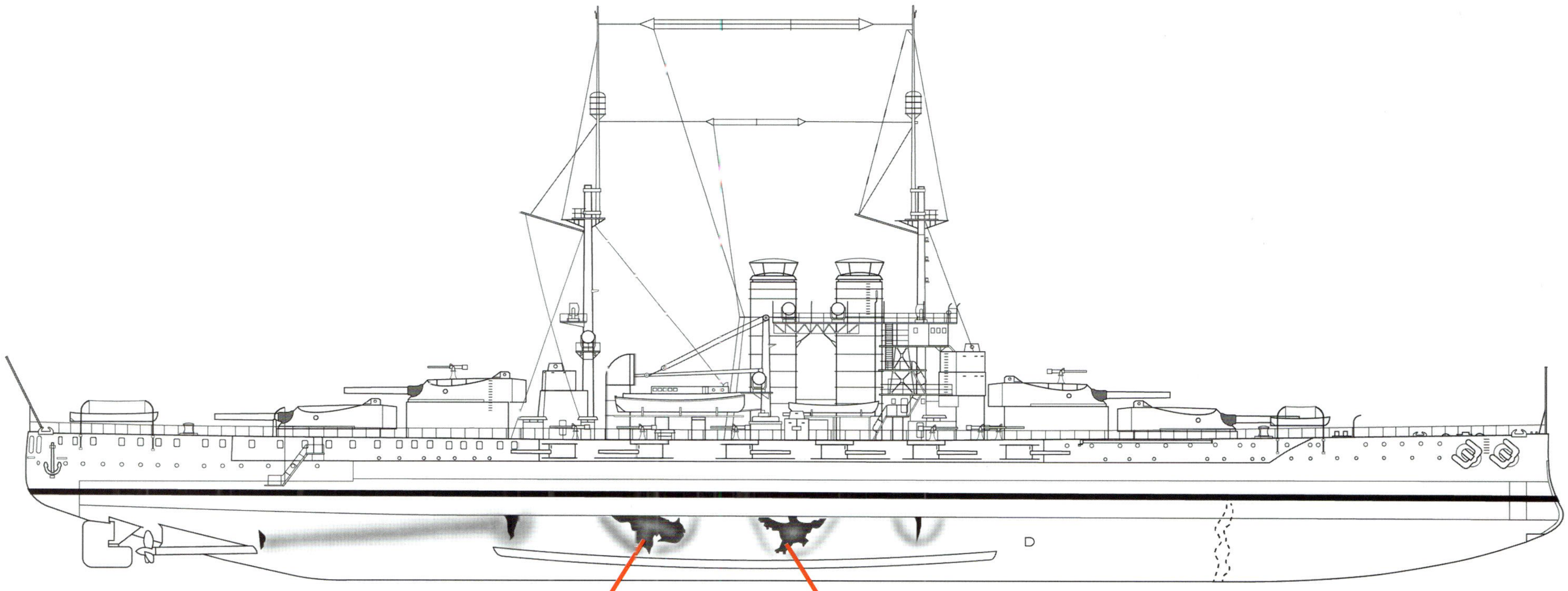

The MAS-15 Italian Navy Torpedo-armed Motorboat – Oleg Pomoshnikov
LUBLIN 2021 • ISBN 978-83-66673-36-6

3D illustrations and captions: **Oleg Pomoshnikov** • Text: **Jan Radziemski** • Text translation: **Stanisław Powała-Niedźwiecki** • Photos: **public domain, WLB Stuttgart** • Design: **KAGERO STUDIO** – Łukasz Maj
KAGERO Publishing • www.kagero.pl, e-mail: kagero@kagero.pl, marketing@kagero.pl
Editorial office, Marketing, Distribution: KAGERO Publishing, Akacjowa 100, os. Borek, Turka, 20-258 Lublin 62, Poland, phone/fax (+48) 81 501 21 05
www.kagero.eu

3D visualisations are based on the available photographs, drawings and other archive data, and should be treated only as author's attempt to recreate the original look of the particular machine as faithfully as possible. If you are in possession of materials to which author did not reach, and you would like to help us to develop a better publication, please contact the Publisher on: redakcja@kagero.pl